House

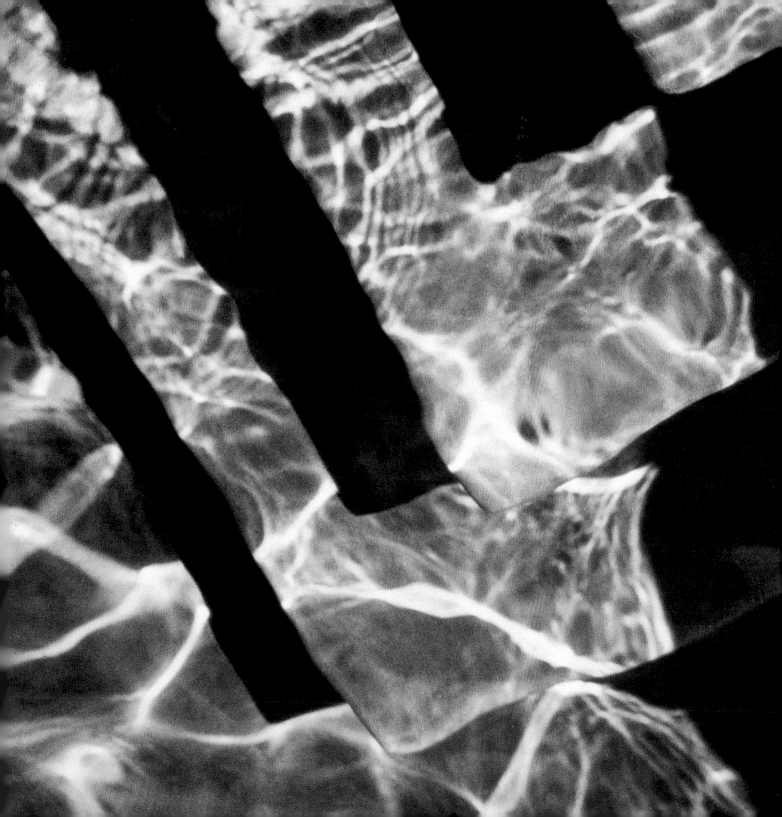

Steven Holl

House

Black Swan Theory

Princeton Architectural Press
New York

House: Black Swan Theory 10

House: Black Swan Theory

The Insignificant
What is more appealing than an azure sky if not the docile clarity of a cloud? This is why I prefer any theory whatsoever to silence, and even more than a blank page a piece of writing that passes as insignificant.

This is my whole exercise, and my health-restoring sigh.
—Francis Ponge[1]

Form to Experience
In the seventeenth century, the study of knowledge—epistemology—first began to replace metaphysics. It was the twentieth century that shattered previous paradigms with modernism in painting, sculpture, architecture, music, dance, and literature. Radical experiments in space-making, free association, and experimentation would later develop into styles. Modern architecture of the house became institutionally formalized (in the Museum of Modern Art's 1932 exhibition The International Style). Necessarily, styles go out of fashion and will be replaced and in turn rejected again (postmodernism, deconstructivism, etc).

Rather than on-going cycles of "isms" and their replacements, the conception of architecture could enter a paradigm shift toward a more open-ended position informed by a phenomenological interrogation. Rather than inherited dualism, the experience of interrelating body, brain, and world could frame and provide for a new position. This three-dimensional triad is always a unique position. Not unlike a scientific paradigm shift, architecture, and especially the architecture of the house, can be seen as a complex phenomenological problem that would benefit from a phenomenological description.

Architects and artists create in an attempt to make people perceive, to make something visible. As an instrument of the experience of time, light, and place, the house has the potential for poetic language and relative autonomy. It has the potential "to speak of something other" that grounds or precedes the architecture.

Nicolas Pople categorized this attitude as "one-off houses" but he elaborates:

> Holl's intention has more than one theoretical position to support it: as described, it is a cosmology which sees architecture as a dynamic process whereby we constantly reinvent our relationship to the world of the senses, including our sense of time and space. This mission has an intention rooted in metaphysics and is a foil to what Holl seems to read as the ever more dominant role of materialistic and scientific thinking and the resulting loss of diversity and specificity in local cultural environments.[2]

As any personal reflection might be prone to retrospective justifications, many have elaborated upon this discussion. As Carole Rifkind indicates:

> Increasingly concerned with architectural theory, Steven Holl

visualized an architecture of strange and mysterious beginnings with the hope of original and unique meanings in each place. Holl's 1991 Stretto House in Dallas broke out of the modernist fold to enter fully into the realm of sensation.[3]

An Ideal Exists in the Specific; An Absolute in the Relative

This book collects houses (built and unbuilt) designed from 1986 to 2006 within the framework of intentions originally outlined in our first book *Anchoring*. Seeking an alternative to ideology-laden works of the time, yet seeking a stance more theoretical than an attitude of linguistic historicism, each house was developed from what we had thought of as a "limited concept." We referred to this position as "Black Swan Theory":

> ... an Architecture based on limited concept begins with dissimilarity and variation. It illuminates the singularity of a specific situation. The universal-to-specific order is inverted to become specific-to-universal.
>
> The critic will observe that this strategy of inversion may become an ideology in itself. This is not the intention here, but even so, this would be an ideology forever changing, a black swan theory, mutable and unpredictable.[4]

How many white swans does one need to observe before inferring that all swans are white and that there are no black swans?

Today the term has taken different meanings. A black swan glossary has been published by Professor Nassim Nicholas Taleb of the "Sciences of Uncertainty" department at the University of Massachusetts, Amherst. Among others, Professor Taleb takes inspiration from Benoit Mandelbrot's methods for thinking about deviations.

Site: Maximum Compression

Maximum compression of architectural thought might yield domestic simplicity in variation in the design of a house. Intensity can be brought to bear on a simple project that forges a manifold relation of place, space, materials, and light. When realized, delight in meditative spaces and inspiring details holds the potential to alter our daily lives.

One house in this collection begins with a musical analogy developing the concept of "stretto" (from a 1937 composition by Béla Bartók) with purely architectonic means. A house on Martha's Vineyard is developed from a particular passage of Herman Melville's *Moby Dick* that takes place on the island. The idea develops from a whale skeleton becoming an exoskeleton balloon frame of typical wooden house construction turned inside-out. Another house on Lake Champlain is raised on the ruins of an eighteenth century nail factory and develops from oblique readings and a skin of cartridge brass. A Long Island house begins in a 1949 Jackson Pollock painting *There Were Seven in Eight*.

Of the fifteen houses in this collection, none can be viewed as typical or prototypical. Each of these houses is an attempt at building into and with the site, an attempt to enhance and reveal its unique qualities. The aim at condensed meanings in these houses is a resolution to illuminate experience and phenomenal dimensions.

Perhaps these houses should have been grouped chronologically, or they could have been grouped according to materiality: wooden houses, concrete-block houses, metal houses, etc. Instead they are ordered according to scale—largest to smallest. As this book is being developed with its counterpart, *Urbanisms*, the two books form a pair. The focus here is on the "micro" scale, in the latter one it is on "macro" scale. One focuses on inner space, the other outer space.

The rural house overlooking ten or more acres might stand like a guard preserving landscape from encroaching sprawl. Around metropolitan centers the rising global tide of sprawl and its "jammed traffic to more freeways to more cars to more pollution" chain reaction has unforeseen consequences. Collectively held natural landscapes and densely packed pedestrian-oriented towns might ensure the continuation and preservation of remaining green forested land.

Porous Light

Natural light is an essential force interlocked with time. The sun arcs through the sky each day at a different angle; the season's change plays out in the vessel of the house like a volumetric sundial.

Unexpected changing intensities and consistencies drive sunlight in the counterpoint of moving shadows. Black against white, blurred against crisp, dissolving against knife-sharp edges, the subtle music of light plays out in space. Porous light and shadow, like the dapple of the sun's rays penetrating dense foliage, is often ordered in elliptical shapes. This phenomenon is due to the fact that the sun is not a point; it is like a sun picture on a sheet of paper.

Shadow, sunlight, and geometry are interlocked in experiential phenomena. Looking at my own shadow on the ground I notice that the shadow of my head is blurry while shadows of my feet are sharp.

The shadow of a porous plane, like the shadows of wire mesh, can exhibit curious properties. For example, a rectangular mesh at certain sun angles only shows vertical shadows. In his 1954 book *Light and Color in the Open Air*, the physicist M. Minnaert writes about nature's phenomena, exclaiming, "It is very difficult to see new things, even when they are before our very eyes."[5]

The distance of the shadow to the plane of its projection drastically alters its character. To see this phenomenon, simply hold a perforated plane immediately in front of a piece of blank paper then move it farther away gradually. If the architect engages this natural light phenomenon, these very different shadow patterns might be created by a certain architectural space.

The phenomenon of doubled shadows can be seen in winter through leafless trees when shadows of two parallel branches are superimposed. When the distant blurry shadow is superimposed on the crisp near one, a bright line can appear in the middle of the sharp shadow. Junichiro Tanizaki's 1977 book *In Praise of Shadows* describes "an inexpressible aura of depth and mystery of faint light. Shadow in traditional Japanese rooms presents an uncertainty... and ... dreamlike luminescence."[6]

The hope of opening our eyes to see the changing phenomena of the light of day and the seasons is a central aim. A clear concept driving geometry, structure, and material shapes new spaces in light. To overcome the prosaic domestic clichés requires a new openness, which can rouse and project inspiration.

Refraction/Reflection/Transparency

The refraction of sunlight by a pool of slightly undulating water is a delightful phenomenon visible in the Stretto House's "Flooded Room" and pool court (1991). To establish the ripples of late afternoon sunlight on the dining room ceiling of the Little Tesseract House, the cooling pond was positioned as a rectangle on the southwest elevation. The visual drama of refracted and reflected sunlight can bring a seasonal and daily change—music to any carefully designed room.

To set a window far back into a wall elevation is to put its glass in shadow—good practice for shading in a south elevation. On the contrary, to project window glass outward on a north elevation is a way of capturing and framing sections of the reflected landscape in the building facade. The north facade windows of the Little Tesseract House are projected out on steel flanges so as to "float" pictures of the adjacent landscape over the patina of the weathering charcoal stucco. Transparency in the soft light of an obscure channel-glass facade can yield a wonderful diffused quality. The shade and shadow pattern created at the transparent entry way of the Planar House is an homage to shadow and shade in the hot Arizona sun.

Light—from the rising sun to the reflection of sunlight off the water to the potential for shadows of moonlight through a skylight—is a major focus in each of the houses in individual ways. The New Mexico sun at the Turbulence House is narrowed into L-shaped slices of skylight at the roof, connecting roof and wall and animating the white curved plaster interior without creating unwanted heat. The linear strips of sunlight that animate the Writing With Light House are exactly at the heart of the idea of that house.

Chromatic Duration: Extended Time

In a domestic setting, color intensity, hue, tone, and saturation need to be taken into account. The extended time spent in living spaces and the possibility of subtle coloration changes occurring from the natural phenomena outside are also important factors in design. For example, the blue-white light reflecting off snow outside requires a white ceiling next to a glass wall to fully appreciate its subtle power. The iridescent glow of sunlight on ice outside a window would go unnoticed without a simple background frame. When an orange-red sunset glows in channel glass, the structural thickness orchestrates a pattern that can only be fully appreciated in a white or off-white surrounding wall. In some situations, a bright exterior color is a site-connective strategy. The red color of the Y House is a link to the ancient lead-red paint used for hundreds of years on barns in the surrounding Catskill Mountains. The interiors in white and natural ash only pick up a pink-red glow from exteriors when the sunlight is in certain positions.

Just as site and circumstance are blank canvases for a fresh look at the form and geometry of a house, so color—or a colorless approach—is always uniquely considered.

Structural Abstraction: Material Potential

These houses are the result of an abstract concept driving a simple geometric operation in an integral relation with the materials of construction. Out of time, they are resolutely modern. The balloon-frame wood construction of the Martha's Vineyard House, aligned with its site concept, becomes an exoskeletal building of linear shadows and developed linear characteristics. Its structure rests delicately on its fragile site; vertical 6x6 columns terminate on point foundations.

The Planar House in Phoenix is structured in tilt-up concrete, exposing its raw, thick, planar structural parts interlocking with the voids, becoming windows. In the hot Arizona sun this structural concrete, with its deeply shadowed, south-facing porch, is cool grey at its temperate best.

On the island of Kauai'i, where it isn't heat but wind force that is the determinate element, the Oceanic Retreat construction is board-formed with green-stained poured-in-place concrete. Due to the persistent rain, the penetrating stain could contain agents to seal the concrete and yet the natural weathering color would merge with surrounding moss green.

The Nail Collector's House in Essex, New York, constructed of a simple plywood diaphragm and frame, is skinned in cartridge brass with stainless steel nail-heads exposed. This recycled economical material has unpredictable natural weathering properties, which allow the house to fuse with the various sun exposures and wind-blown facades unique to the site.

Proportion: Number, Scale, and Intuition

What Lucioli Pacioli called the "Divine Proportion" and what Leonardo da Vinci called the "Golden Section" in modern scientific life continues as the ratio 1:1.618, comparable only to 3.14 in its irrational number magic. All the houses in this collection were subject to proportional adjustment according to a "fine tuner" relating the main proportions to 1:1.618. You might say they are all Golden Section houses; like a piece of music, their spaces have a volumetric harmony that is played out in different ways depending on the entering light and the passing of time and the seasons.

Ideas and numbers have always been at the core of architecture. For the Greeks, proportion—which they called "analogia"—achieves consonance between the whole and every part. Epinomis argued that "numbers are the highest degree of knowledge."

In his seminal 1946 book *The Geometry of Art and Life,* Matila Ghyka connects Greek and Gothic canons of proportion to the harmonious growth geometry of the logarithmic spiral in flowers, shells, living organisms, and crystal lattices.[7] The "Golden Section" defined by $(1 + 5)/2 = 1.618$ is one of the most remarkable algebraic numbers. Theodore Cook addresses this ratio in his book *The Curves of Life,* and he demonstrates its multiple qualities for living organisms.[8] It is found in the distribution of branches in trees, leaves, seeds, etc. More recent scientific investigation found this ratio in the solar wind.

With today's computer-charged design and fabrication, key numbers of proportional relations might find new projective geometric and spatial relations. However it is not a matter of automatically inserting ratios into digital processes. Scale, space, and form in any architectural composition must be guided by intuition.

Cyclical Thermal Mass

Maximizing natural energy has been our concern since the construction of a passive solar house in Manchester, Washington, in 1974. The most successful experiment has been the Solar Stack wall of the Little Tesseract in Rhinebeck, New York, 2001. The eighteen-foot wall of south-facing channel glass heats the upper studio to 75 degrees on a sunny winter day with outside temperature at 15 or 20 degrees. Alternately, in the summer, with upper cavity flaps open and pond cooling intakes open, cool air circulates over the special adjacent water pond, cooling the cavity considerably. If the sun is stronger, more air is drawn in over the pond, resulting in more cooling.

The high electricity rates in Hawaii and the fact that the islands run on dirty coal-fired plants prompted an HVAC design for the Oceanic Retreat completely powered by a roof array of advanced P.V. cells.

Previously New and New Building Techniques

The definition of constructional elements in new technologies carries house design into the twenty-first century. New integral forms begin from construction. There were no tilt-up concrete constructed houses in Paradise Valley, Arizona, but now, even before our Planar House has been completed, others are using this technique. The Turbulence House was digitally driven prefabricated construction. Drawings went from New York computers to the Kansas City manufacturer Zahner & Co. with the first 32-piece shell being assembled for an exhibition in the Palladio Basilica in Vicenza, 2002. For the second addition at Abiquiu, New Mexico, the 32 parts from Kansas City were bolted together on a site-poured concrete slab. Local craftsmen completed the interiors in New Mexican natural plasterwork with Santa Fe curved techniques. Steel work in raw local steel with exposed welds further connects this house in material and spatial feeling to its desert mesa site.

Parallax Inversions in Space
Parallax is the dynamic change of spatial volumes due to the moving position of the body as it experiences space. The house is not an object; it is experienced in a dynamic relationship with the terrain, the angle of approach, the sky, and light, with focus on internal axes of movement. The change in the arrangement of surfaces defining space due to the change in position of a viewer is the essence of parallax. Spatial definition is ordered by angles of perception. The idea of a facade is too limiting. The angle of movement, organized by the path, forces a spatial definition with the body engaging the stationary building. This line of movement engages the other dynamic forces of sun and shadow and the reflectivity or transparency of materials. When we pass into or through a small building, the exhilaration of interior perspectives open up, close, shift, and open up again. Even in a small house we can experience an exhilaration of overlapping perspectives while interlocked in a web of relationships with movement, parallax, and light.

Condensed Meanings
One of the most immediate vehicles to advance the experiment that a building can be a spatial representation of an idea is the small house. While this intellectual hope drives the design process, the interior experience of the realized construction is its larger aim. The joy of living receives new zest, new awareness, and new perceptions within inspired interior spaces.

The project of a house is one of architecture's immediately accessible doors to the poetic language of space. In the present is its daily zeal, a container for the day's light from the pale yellow of dawn to the deep blue of twilight. The house is a box for the existential objects of life. It is a vessel for the imagination, for laughter and emotion and a silent place for the poetic, a room of reverie.

Anchoring
Today we must reinvent *Anchoring*—new communications, new global views, new technologies, changing spaces—and are forced to make even more critical the concept.

Architecture is bound to situation. Unlike music, painting, sculpture, film and literature, a construction (non-mobile) is intertwined with the experience of a place. The site of a building is more than a mere ingredient in this conception. It is its physical and metaphysical foundation.

The resolution of the functional aspects of site and building, the vistas, sun angles, circulation, and access are the basic "physics" that demand the "metaphysics" of architecture. Through a link, an extended motive, a building is more than something merely fashioned for the site.

Building transcends physical and functional requirements by fusing with a place, by gathering the meaning of a situation. Architecture does not so much intrude on a landscape as it serves to explain it. Illumination of a site is not a simplistic replication of its "context"; to reveal an aspect of a place may not confirm its "appearance." Hence the habitual ways of seeing may well be interrupted.

Architecture and site should have an experiential connection, a metaphysical link, a poetic link. When a work of architecture successfully fuses a building and situation, a third condition emerges. In this third entity denotation and connotation merge; expression is linked to idea, which is joined to site. The suggestive and implicit are manifold aspects of an intention.

A building has one site. In this one situation, its intentions are collected. Building and site have been interdependent since the beginning of architecture. In the past this connection was manifest without conscious intention through the use of local materials and craft and by an association of the landscape

with events of history and myth. Today the link between site and architecture must be found in new ways, which are part of a constructive transformation in modern life.[9]

Anchoring; the criticality of this concept has become even more evident as architects continue to work internationally. Currently we focus on works under construction in Beijing, Nanjing, and in Shenzhen (China). With further work going on in Copenhagen and Herning (Denmark), Biarritz (France), Beirut (Lebanon), and at Lake Garda (Italy), along with several sites in the United States. Anchoring a work of architecture to its site in this world, the specific climate, culture, and immediate site history becomes an urgent argument. Any architect caught up with the current speed and globalization of today's architecture realizes that this is an unprecedented time in the history of architecture: requiring an unprecedented philosophical commitment.

Unless an architect is willing to depreciate his or her works by recycling designs regardless of site, culture, and circumstance, the challenge of extremely diverse lands, cultures, and climates and their urban conditions set unparalleled obligations for architecture today. Reflected in the collection of these diverse houses, a theory reversing specific to universal— a black swan theory—suggests an aim for larger, more complex building types. A twenty-first century position that strives to reframe the inherited dualism of the last century's suffixes might spark a paradigm shift toward a new focus on architecture's potential to shape experience, interrelating body, brain, and world.

1. Francis Ponge, *Selected Poems*, ed. Margaret Guiton (Winston-Salem, N.C.: Wake Forest University Press, 1994), 12.

2. Nicolas Pople, *Experimental Houses* (London: Calman & King, Ltd., 2002), 199.

3. Carole Rifkind, *A Field Guide to Contemporary Architecture* (New York: Plume Books, 1998), 50.

4. Steven Holl, *Anchoring* (New York: Princeton Architectural Press, 1988), 12.

5. M. G. J. Minnaert, *Light and Colour in the Open Air*, trans. H. M. Krenner-Priest (London: G. Bell and Sons Ltd., 1959), vi.

6. Junichiro Tanizaki, *In Praise of Shadows* (New Haven, Conn.: Leete's Island Books, 1977), 21.

7. Matila Ghyka, *The Geometry of Art and Life* (New York: Sheed and Ward, 1946), 124–55.

8. Theodore Cook, *The Curves of Life: Being an Account of Spiral Formations and Their Application to Growth in Nature, to Science and to Art: with Special Reference to the Manuscripts of Leonardo da Vinci* (New York: H. Holt, 1914), 88.

9. Steven Holl, *Anchoring*, 9.

The Swiss Residence

This scheme placed first in the competition of ten Swiss-American teams' designs for the replacement of the Washington, D.C., residence of the Swiss Ambassador.

It is not only a private house but also a cultural gathering place on which the standards and self-image of a country are measured.

Sited on a hill with a direct view through the trees to the Washington Monument in the distance, a diagonal line of overlapping spaces drawn through a cruciform courtyard plan was the conceptual starting point. Official arrival spaces and ceremony spaces are connected along this diagonal line on the first level, while private living functions are on the level above.

Materials are charcoal-colored concrete trimmed in local slate and sand-blasted structural glass planks.

Constructed according to Swiss "Minergie Standard," the south facades use passive solar energy. The roof is sedum green.

The existing natural landscape is clarified with new trees, while the plateau of the residence defines an arrival square, a reception courtyard, and an herb garden in an urban precinct.

opposite
Entrance court

right
View of Washington Monument

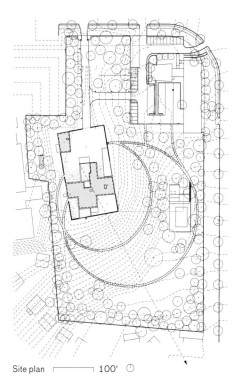

Site plan   100'

top
Charcoal-stained concrete and white grass: a memory of the ice and snow against rock in the Swiss Alps

bottom
Model

opposite
A lake-like pool within the courtyard

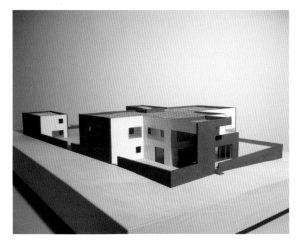

right
Diagonal cuts through overlapping orthogonal spaces

opposite, top
Main entry hall

opposite, bottom
Stairway to ambassador's private space and guest rooms

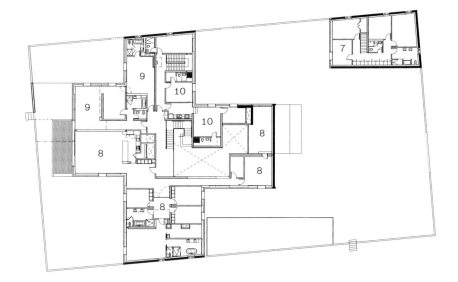

Second-floor plan

First-floor plan ⊢——⊣ 20' ⊕

1 Main entrance hall
2 Dining and recreation
3 Service
4 Herb garden
5 Reception terrace
6 Reflecting pool
7 Caretaker house
8 Private quarter
9 Guests
10 Staff

above
Green sedum roof

right
**View of entry from
living level**

opposite
Reflecting pond

Stretto House

Situated adjacent to spring-fed ponds served by existing concrete dams, the Stretto House projects the character of the site in a series of concrete block spatial dams with a metal-framed aqueous space flowing through them. Flowing over the dams, like the overlapping stretti in music, water is an overlapping reflection of the space of the landscape outside as well as the virtual overlapping of the spaces inside.

The form of the house parallels a particular score rich in stretti: Bartók's *Music for Strings, Percussion, and Celeste.* In four movements, the piece divides distinctly between heavy (percussion) and light (strings). Where music has a materiality in instrumentation and sound, this architecture attempts a similar relationship:

$$\frac{material \times sound}{time} = \frac{material \times light}{space}$$

The building is formed in four sections, each consisting of two modes: heavy orthogonal masonry and light curvilinear metal. The concrete block and metal recall Texas vernacular. While the plan is purely orthogonal, the section is curvilinear. The guest house inverts this scheme with a curvilinear plan and orthogonal section,

similar to the inversions of the subject in the first movement of the Bartók score. In the main house aqueous space is developed by several means: floor planes pull the level of one space through to the next, roof planes pull space over walls, and an arched wall pulls light down from a skylight. Materials and details continue the spatial concepts in poured concrete, glass cast in fluid shapes, slumped glass, and liquid terrazzo.

Arriving at the space via a driveway bridging over the stream, a visitor passes through the overlapping spaces of the house, glimpsing the flanking gardens and arriving at an empty room flooded by the existing pond. The room, doubling its space in reflection and opening both to the site and the house, becomes the asymmetrical center of two sequences of aqueous space and is the connecting point between the literal aqueous space— the pools of water outside the house— and the philosophical aqueous space.

right
Early concept sketch

opposite
The flooded room reflected in the existing pond

Site plan 50'

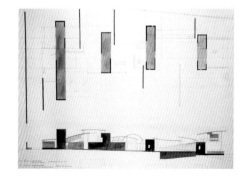

above
Models

opposite
The prefabricated magnetic induction-pipe structure gives the roof its shape.

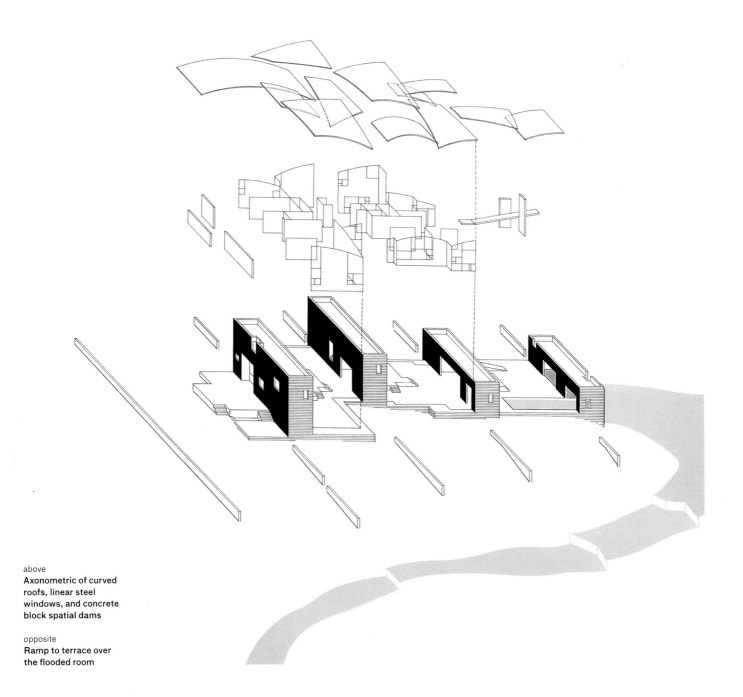

above
**Axonometric of curved
roofs, linear steel
windows, and concrete
block spatial dams**

opposite
**Ramp to terrace over
the flooded room**

left
**Melting ice fountain
at entry**

right
Existing pond

opposite
**Reflections on ceiling
of flooded room**

1 Garage
2 Entry
3 Living room
4 Art storage room
5 Library
6 Study
7 Dining room
8 Breakfast area
9 Kitchen
10 Walled garden
11 Pool
12 Flooded room
13 Bedroom
14 Sitting room
15 Roof terrace

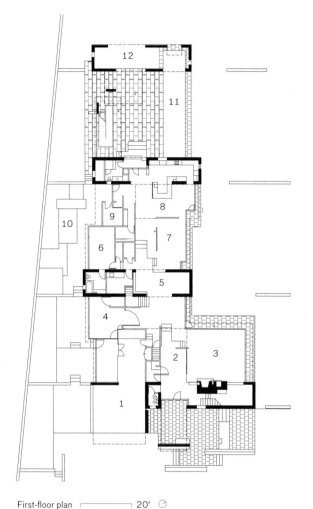

First-floor plan ⊢————⊣ 20' ⊘

Second-floor plan

opposite
**Fluid terrazzo floor
pours through**

above
**Bronze entry handle on
reddened brass door**

opposite
**Entry hall and living
room**

left
Curved window in library

right
Guest house

opposite
The flooded room

Writing With Light House

The concept of this linear wooden beach house evolved from the inspiration of the site's close proximity to the studio of the painter Jackson Pollock. Several free-form designs were made based on the 1949 painting *There Were Seven in Eight*. Opening up the interior to the free expanse of the bay and the north view of the Atlantic Ocean required closing the south side for privacy from the street.

The final scheme brackets the internal energy into an open frame, which the sun shines through in projecting lines. The strips of white light inscribe and seasonally bend internal spaces dynamically with the cycle of the day.

The wooden balloon frame construction is comparable to the strip-wood sand dune fencing along the ocean. Several guest rooms swirl around the double-level living room from which one ascends to a pool suspended over the garage. From this upper pool court, the distant ocean is visible.

right
Early concept sketches

opposite
Pool court over garage visible through cedar slats

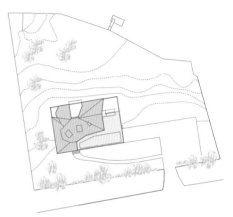

Site plan ⌐——⌐ 20' ◔

top
View from the bay

bottom
Model

opposite
**Stairway to swimming
pool deck**

right
Stairway to bedrooms

opposite, right
Strips of sunlight move throughout the day.

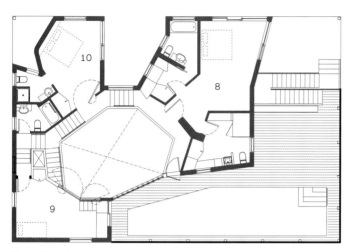

1 Entry
2 Living
3 Kitchen
4 Dining
5 Library
6 Guest 1
7 Garage
8 Master bedroom
9 Guest 2
10 Guest 3

Second-floor plan

First-floor plan └────────┐ 10' ⊕

above and right
Views of arrival alcove

opposite, right
**Views from dining room
with double-fronted
fireplace; concrete floor
the color of wet sand**

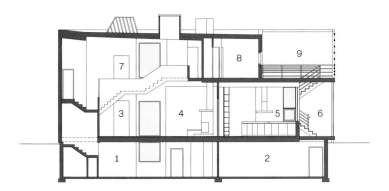

West–east section

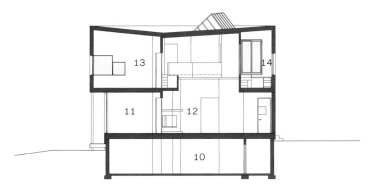

South–north section ⌐————⌐ 10'

1 Basement
2 Utility room
3 Library beyond
4 Living
5 Kitchen
6 Kitchen porch
7 Guest 3 beyond
8 Master bath
9 Pool porch
10 Basement
11 Library
12 Living
13 Guest 3
14 Guest 4

above
View from pool deck

opposite
**Screened porch at
kitchen**

above, left
**Ocean at distant east
horizon**

above, right, and opposite
**Entry elevation screens
interior for privacy from
Flying Point Road**

Oceanic Retreat

The site on the northwest prow of Kauai'i, Hawaii, prone to extremely strong winds, is on the leading edge of a tectonic Pacific Ocean plate which has moved across a volcanic hot spot at a constant rate of 3.5 inches per year. An imaginary datum, parallel to the horizon, strikes the mass of the concrete house, which is then carved out below for the best views and flow of space. Like two continents separated by tectonic shift, the imaginary erosion forms two L-shaped forms, one a guest house. The crenellated section of the large room in the main house is in increments of 3.5 inches (one year/ one step). Roofs of the stained-concrete structures are covered in photovoltaic solar panels, which reverse meter into the Kauai'i power grid. The lap pool courtyard terracing is built of volcanic stone from near the site.

After the horizontal datum, space is like water; the plan and section contains, drops, embanks, and then releases the space down the curvilinear path through the natural gardens and finally to the ocean.

top
Map of Hawaiian Islands showing volcanic hot spots (red dots) and direction of tectonic plate movement

bottom
Concept sketch

opposite
View from Ocean Beach, Kauai'i

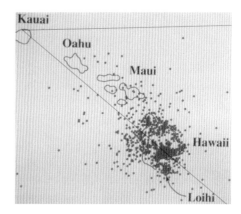

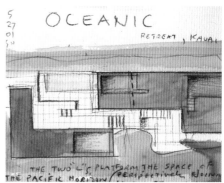

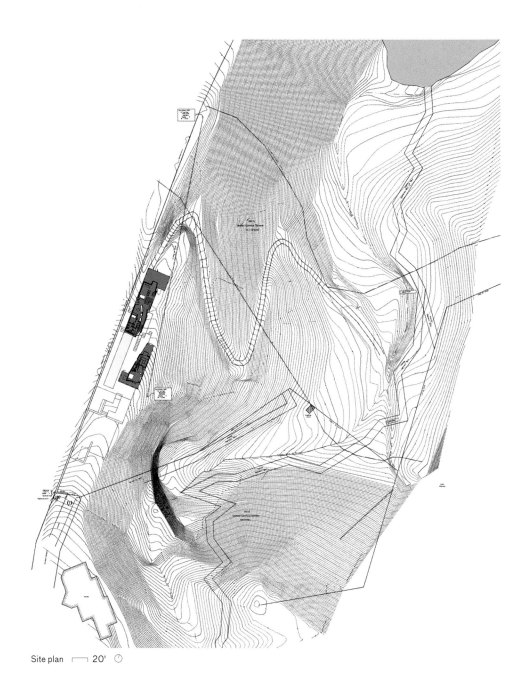

right
Site plan with Ocean Beach

opposite
Guest and main houses envelop a courtyard

Site plan ⌐ 20' ⊘

right and opposite, top
Moss green stained-concrete structure exposed

opposite, right
Concept sketch

CONCEPT!

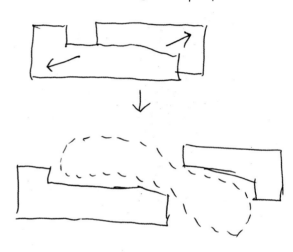

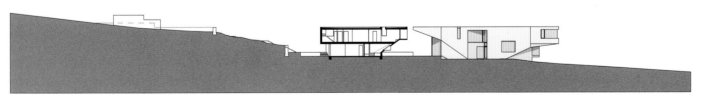

South–north section ⌐————⌐ 20'

1 Lap pool
2 Dining
3 Studio
4 Guest
5 Living
6 Kitchen
7 Guest
8 Yoga

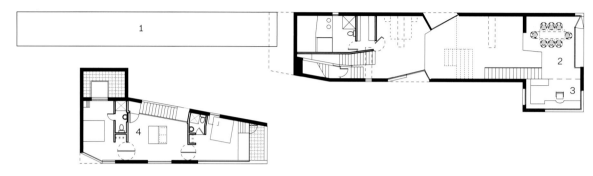

Second-floor plan

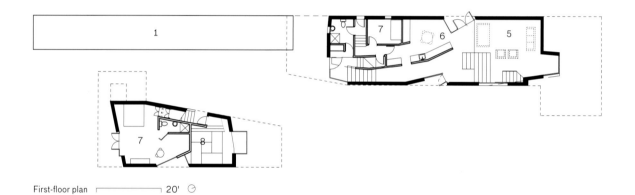

First-floor plan ⌐————————⌐ 20' ◔

opposite
**Pacific horizon view;
solar cells cover roof of
house and guest house**

Porosity House

The physics of light is evident in shadows. The boundary between light and shadow—usually the gray area of "penumbra"—is filled with the mysteries of the mathematics of light. Arguments for the fusion of architecture, urbanism, and landscape can be reinforced with a testament for the fusion of spirit and matter as well as fusion of light with form, shade, and shadow. Natural light and shadow have the psychological power to inspire and encourage. The speed of shadow is vibrant. When the seasonal change of the sun angle is multiplied by variations from sunrise to sunset, porosity, when fused with light, attains choreographic phenomena.

This Long Island, New York site—adjacent to the busy road connecting Watermill and the Hamptons—embraces the concept of porosity. For this two-family weekend retreat, a central inner pool courtyard is the point of focus. Protected from highway sound and catching south sun, this courtyard is like a little urban precinct.

Existing large trees are to be saved via cut-outs in the plan. Each elevation is developed in screened outdoor porches that were specially requested by the owner. Every sleeping room has an adjacent large porch, totaling

nine in all. They are screened outdoor rooms furnished in wicker. The wood frame structure is sheathed in white-stained cedar boards complemented by water jet–cut marine plywood, also stained white. These porous water jet–cut walls provide the armature to hold screens for the porches. Along the highway edge an 18-inch-wide sound-absorbing fence is constructed in a similar white porous material.

right
Concept sketch

opposite
Pool court

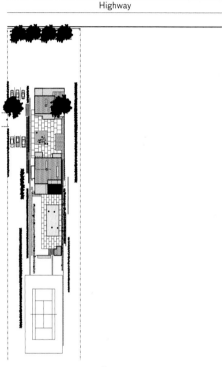

Highway

Site plan ⌐────⌐ 50'

1 Entry
2 Reception
3 Dining
4 Living
5 Kitchen
6 Breakfast
7 Bedroom
8 Maid area
9 Porch

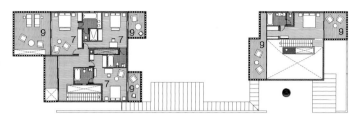

Second-floor plan

First-floor plan

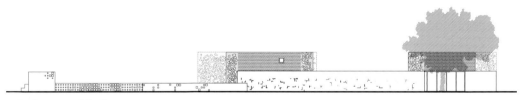

Section ⌐⌐ 20' ◔

opposite
**South facade,
porosity detail, and
soundproof wall**

Sun Slice House

This weekend house on Lake Garda
for an Italian lighting company owner and
his family is organized to frame slices
of sunlight. While the owner's profession
revolves around artificial light, slices
of natural light and their change in space
throughout the day and year is the focus
of the house.

While south elevations are simple
rectangles strategically sliced and
cut for the play of light within, the north
facade is made entirely of glass with
views of Lake Garda.

In order to emphasize the bends and
changes in the strips of sunlight, simple
cubic volumes form the basic building
geometry. These are loosely joined in
topological sheet rubber–like geometry,
which also inscribes wind-protected
courts on both sides of the house.
Changes of season and weather allow
different courtyard opportunities.

The steel frame and concrete structure is skinned with an alloy of copper,
steel, chromium, and nickel, which
weathers to a leathery red color. Interiors
are white plaster with terrazzo floors
on the ground level while bamboo floors
cover the second. Natural ventilation
and geothermal heating and cooling are
part of the energy plan.

right
Concept watercolors

opposite
**View with Lake Garda
in distance**

Site location with Lake Garda

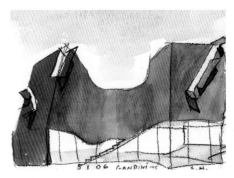

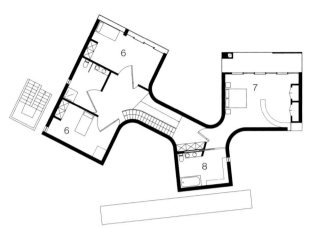

Second-floor plan

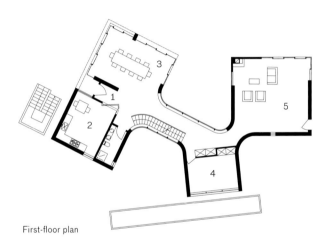

First-floor plan

Basement plan   ⊢——⊣ 5'   ◷

1 Entry
2 Kitchen
3 Dining
4 Studio
5 Living
6 Bedroom
7 Master bedroom
8 Master bathroom
9 Garage
10 Storage
11 Technical space

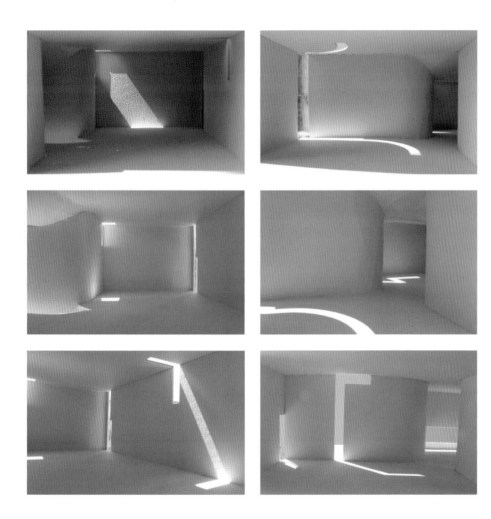

above
**Model studies of sun
slice movement**

opposite
**Model studies of
exterior**

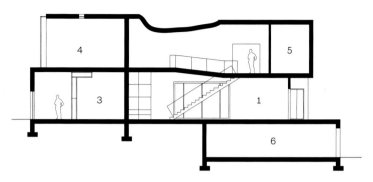

East–west section

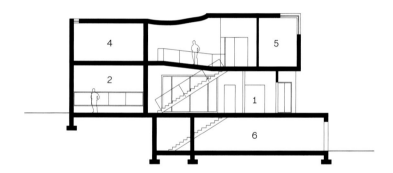

South–east section ⌐━━━━┐ 2'

1 Entry
2 Studio
3 Living
4 Master bedroom
5 Bathroom
6 Garage

above
Exterior studies

opposite
**Facade detail with
sliding sunlight**

Y House

On a hilltop site of eleven acres with a panoramic view to the Catskill Mountains toward the south, the Y House continues the ascent of the hill thrust into balconies splitting into a "Y." The slow passing of time from early morning to sunset is to be a primary experience in the house as different areas become activated with the movement of the sun. The geometry allows sun and shadows to "chase still time."

The Y, like a found forked stick, makes a primitive mark on the vast site extending its view in several directions. The geometry of the Y contains a sectional flip of public/private or day/night zones. On the north half, the day zone is above and night zone below while the south half is reversed. All of these are joined in section by a central Y ramp.

The house occupies the hill and site through three primary relationships: in the ground, on the ground, and over the ground. The portion over the ground is suspended, cantilevered above the portion in the ground, which opens to a stone court.

Various slopes of the metal roof channel rainwater to a single water cistern to the north of the house. A passive solar collection of winter sun occurs through the south glazing, protected from summer sun by its deep porches.

right
Concept sketches

opposite
Branching form from one-story entry

Steel framing and steel roof are iron-oxide red, siding is red-stained cedar, while interiors are white with ash floors.

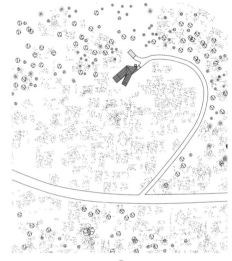

Site plan ⊢——⊣ 100' ◷

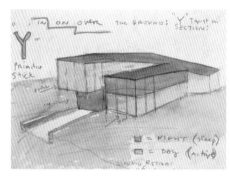

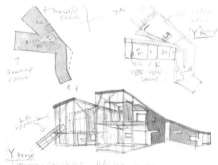

1 Living room
2 Master bedroom
3 Lower foyer
4 Foyer
5 Bedroom
6 Dining room
7 Veranda
8 Reflecting pool

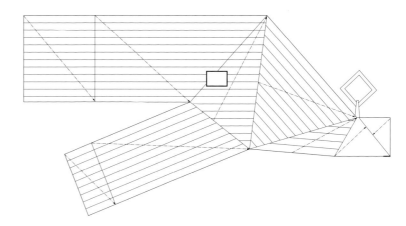

Roof plan

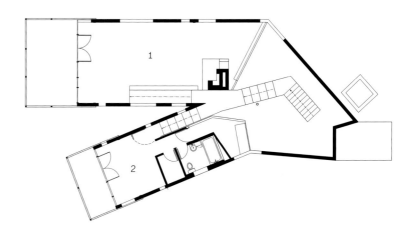

Second-floor plan

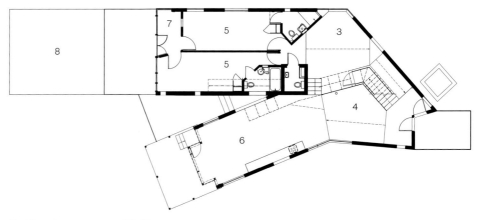

First-floor plan ⊢————┐ 10' ⊖

right
**Living-room porch over
bedroom terrace**

opposite
**Y space catches
the sun**

right
Double door entry

opposite
Y ramp to living room

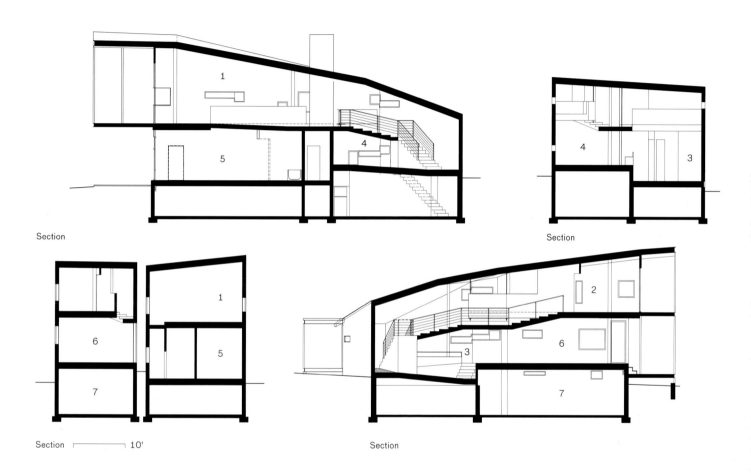

Section

Section

Section |⎯⎯⎯⎯| 10'

Section

1 Living room
2 Master bedroom
3 Lower foyer
4 Foyer
5 Bedroom
6 Dining room
7 Basement

opposite
Kitchen and Y stair

right
View to Catskills

opposite, left
Rain scupper

opposite, right
Folded windows

right
Bent-glass corner

opposite
South elevation

86

Planar House

Sited in Paradise Valley with a direct vista to Camelback Mountain, this house is to be a part of, and vessel for, a large contemporary art collection. Great twentieth-century works by Bruce Nauman, Robert Ryman, and Jannis Kounellis are part of the collection, which includes important video artworks.

Constructed of tilt-up concrete, the nature of the walls merges with the simple orthogonal requirements of the interiors for art.

Light and air chimneys connected to cooling pools articulate the planar geometry. From a courtyard experienced at the entry sequence, a ramp leads to a rooftop sculpture garden—a place of silence and reflection.

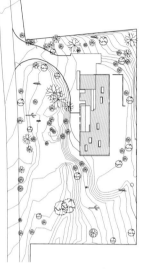

Site plan ⌐——⌐ 50' ◷

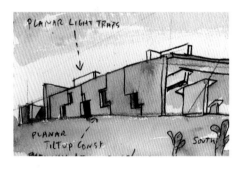

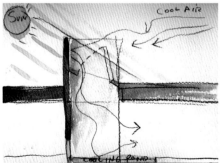

right
Concept sketches

opposite
**Ramp from pool court
to rooftop**

above, left
North facade

above, right
Main entry at courtyard

opposite
South porch

above
**Sun screen of laser-cut
steel at entry**

opposite
Main entry door

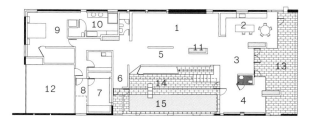

First-floor plan

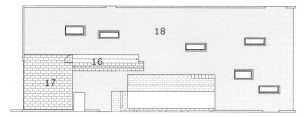

Roof plan ⌐————┐ 22' ⊖

1 Living
2 Kitchen
3 Dining
4 Study
5 Gallery
6 Entry
7 Library
8 Outdoor court
9 Bedroom
10 Bathroom
11 Cool pool
12 Garage
13 Camelback porch
14 Pool court
15 Lap pool
16 Ramp to sculpture terrace
17 Sculpture terrace
18 Terrace

right
Interior at entry

opposite, clockwise
from top left
**Main exhibition space,
cool pools, kitchen
cabinet detail, door
handle, library**

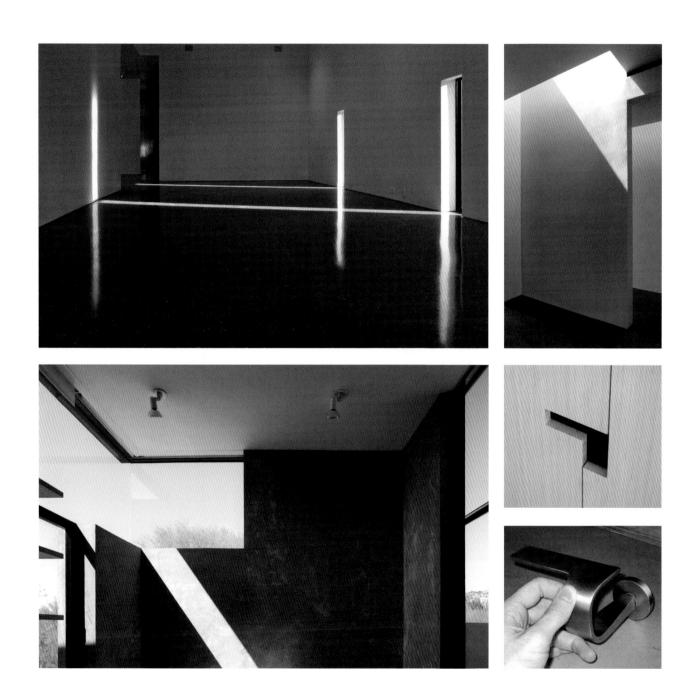

right
Ramp to roof

opposite
Pool court

following spread
Porous light

House at Martha's Vineyard

The site is a hill overlooking the Atlantic Ocean as it meets the Vineyard Sound. A strict planning code determines that the house must be set back from the marshland as well as from a no-build zone on a hill and that it should have a one-story elevation when viewed from the beach.

In the locally inspired novel *Moby Dick*, Herman Melville describes an Indian tribe that made a unique type of dwelling on the island. Finding a beached whale skeleton, they would pull it up to dry land and stretch skins or bark over it, transforming it into a house.

Elevated over the undisturbed natural landscape, the house is like an inside-out balloon-frame structure: the wooden "bones" of the frame carry an encircling veranda, which affords continuous ocean views. Along this porch, wood members receive the natural vines of the island, which transform the straight linear mode of the architecture.

The plan is a simple set of rooms set perpendicular to the view within the setback lines of the site. Beginning with a mud and recreation room off the entry, there are two bedrooms, a kitchen, and a dining room in a protective bay. The living room drops down according to the site. The structural frame, exposed inside and out, meets the undisturbed sand dune on point foundations rather than the more common perimeter footing. The house is clad in a natural weathered gray wood. Roofing is composed of a rubber membrane unrolled over the frame, analogous to the skins over the whale skeleton.

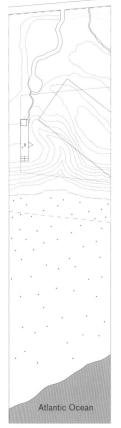

Site plan ⊢———⊣ 100' ⟲

Atlantic Ocean

right
**Original concept sketch
with Melville stamp**

opposite
**Gravel foot path
approach**

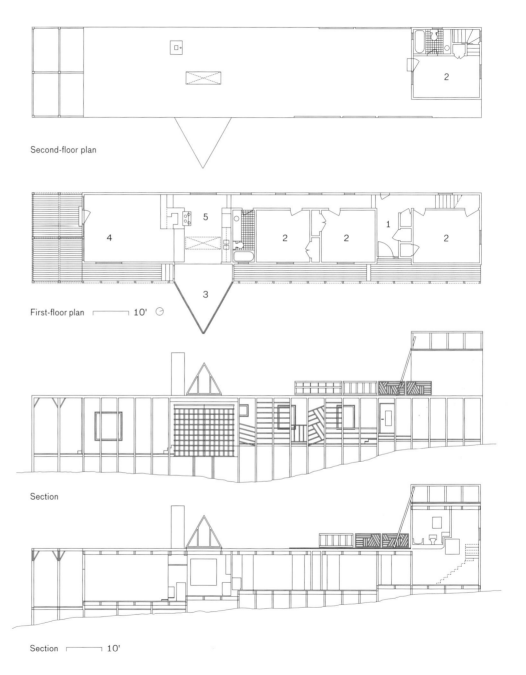

Second-floor plan

First-floor plan ⌐‾‾‾‾‾⌐ 10' ⊘

1 Entry
2 Bedroom
3 Dining room
4 Living
5 Kitchen

Section

above
Skeleton shadows

opposite
West facade

Section ⌐‾‾‾‾‾⌐ 10'

Concept:

WOOD
EXOSKELETON

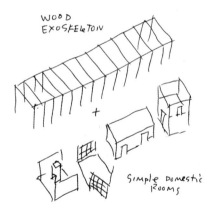

+

SIMPLE DOMESTIC
ROOMS

top
Planar glass lamp

bottom
Concept sketch

right
**Kitchen stove cut into
fireplace**

opposite
View into dining room

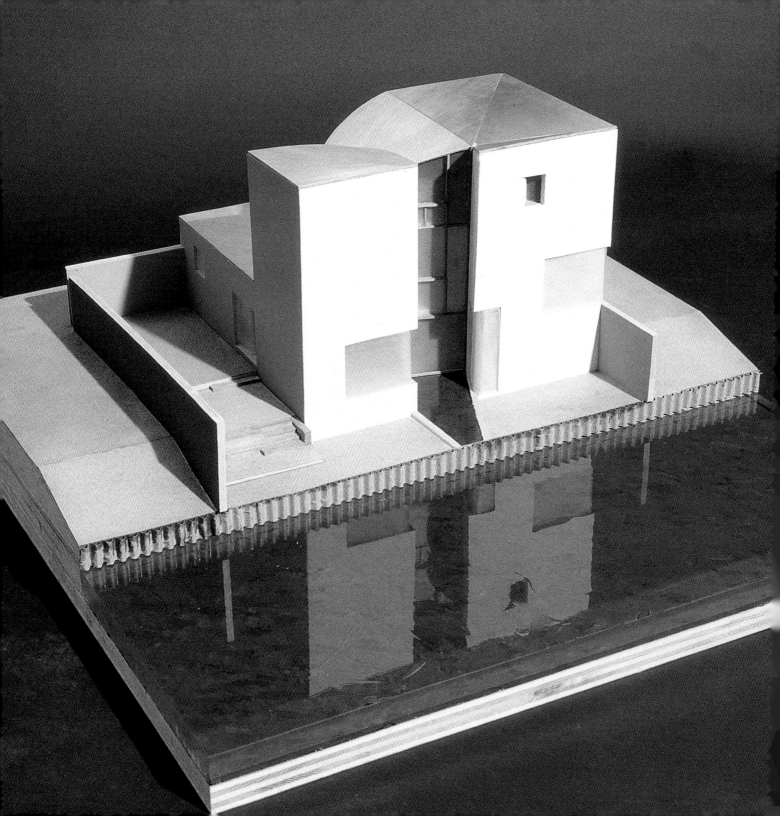

Implosion Villa

Sited on the edge of a canal, the villa is part of a group of eight villas by eight different architects. Rather than emphasize the house as an object, the courtyards are proposed to maximize the outdoor areas in a variety of spaces.

The Implosion Villa is an inversion of the modern courtyard house type, one in which interior space is thrust outward by large panes of glass and walls that continue with the same material into the garden. In this villa, courtyard space implodes: exterior spaces are pulled inward, making fissures into the body of the building. The fissures are warped counter-clockwise into the body of the house beginning at the entrance court.

The counter-clockwise rotation of four courtyards picks up the clockwise rotation of the sun over and around the building, maximizing reflected light. The muted colors of the stained exterior brick are projected by the sun through the fissures into an interior of white plaster and white woodwork. Windows of bent glass chart the inward sucking of space in detail. Rubber floors and high-gloss white ceilings draw the outside light in reflection.

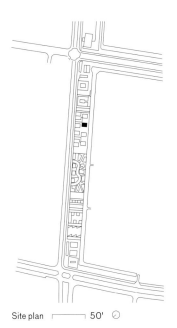

Site plan ⊢——⊣ 50'

right
Concept sketch

opposite
Courtyard opens to canal edge

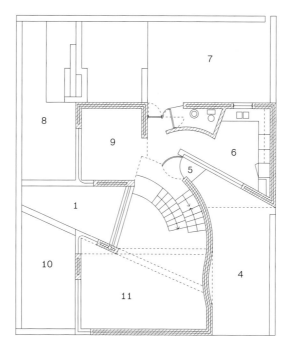

First-floor plan

1 Water court
2 Studio
3 Utility
4 Entry court
5 Entry
6 Kitchen
7 Kitchen court
8 Garden
9 Dining room
10 Garden
11 Living room

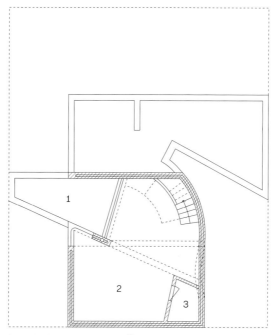

Lower-level plan ⊢——⊣ 5' ◔

opposite
Implosion within walls

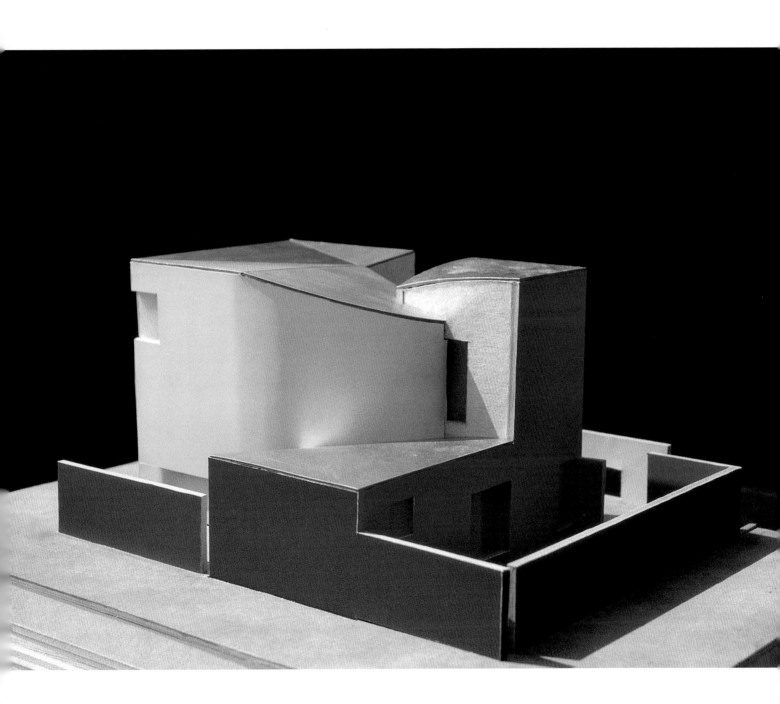

Little Tesseract

A hollow charcoal cube is warped by distorting forces opening a triangle of light from above. This cubic wooden structure is linked by an exoskeletal steel "L" to an existing stone "U." The link, like a porch, is a temperate zone with operable glass. From the central room of the stone U, one moves down a slight ramp in the steel L; space then overlaps diagonally, connecting upward toward the triangle of light. This central spatial connection fuses outwardly contrasting materials.

A solar-stack wall in structural glass planks heats the cube in winter and cools via stack effect in summer. PV cells assist the electrical expenditure. Steel windows slice through the dark stucco on steel plate blades, forming special viewing frames from the interior with unified white plaster heads/jambs/sills.

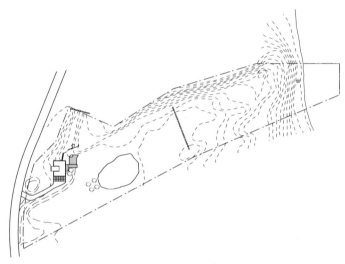

Site plan ⌐——⌐ 50' ⊘

right
Concept sketch showing winning entry for Cornell School of Architecture as compared to Little Tesseract House

opposite
The new facade of the three-part building

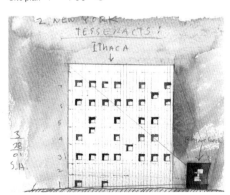

111

right
View from west

opposite, left
View from pond

opposite, right
Steel L and Black Tesseract cube

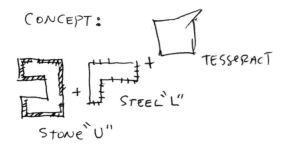

CONCEPT:

STONE "U" + STEEL "L" + TESSERACT

top
**Model: Stone U,
Steel L, Black
Tesseract cube**

bottom
Concept sketch

right
**Steel blade–extruded
windows**

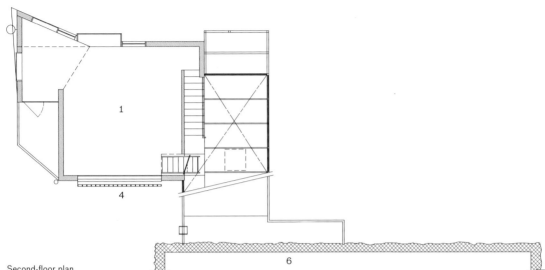

1 Studio
2 Bedroom
3 Dining
4 Solar-stack wall
5 Cooling pond
6 Existing stone U

Second-floor plan

First-floor plan ⌐———⌐ 5' ◷

left
View from dining room

right
Existing trees preserved

opposite
**Stairway to painting
studio**

left
**Steel channel 3½ ×
3½-inch steel tube
structure**

opposite
**Solar-stack wall and
cooling pond**

Nail Collector's House

Overlooking the expanse of Lake Champlain in the nineteenth-century town of Essex, New York, this 1,200-square-foot (111-square-meter) house for a writer is sited on a former nail factory's foundation. The owner has a collection of antique square-head nails gathered over the years on this site.

Windows in the house correspond to the twenty-four chapters of Homer's *Odyssey* and are organized to project "fingers of light" into the interior volume. The main northeast wall has fourteen windows; the southeast and southwest walls contain five windows; and the northwest wall is blank.

The largely open interior ascends counter-clockwise through a series of spaces pierced by the light of the windows. A "prow" thrust toward Lake Champlain completes this upward spiral of space.

White plaster walls, hickory floors, and "cartridge brass" siding nailed in pattern over a wood frame create a tactile weathering for this structure, a poetic reinterpretation of the industrial history of the site and the pre–Civil War architecture of Essex.

right
Watercolor concept drawing

opposite
Sheathing of cartridge brass with exposed walls

Site plan

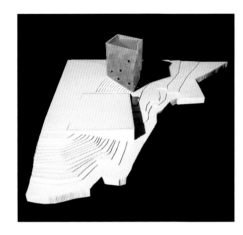

above
Model

right
Pivoting front door

opposite
**Autumn leaves and
cartridge-brass skin**

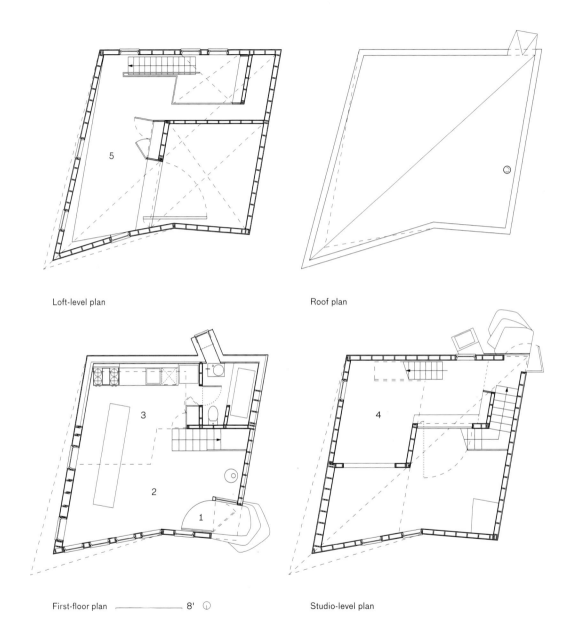

1 Entry
2 Living
3 Kitchen
4 Studio
5 Loft

Loft-level plan

Roof plan

First-floor plan ——————— 8'

Studio-level plan

opposite
**View from the top of the
spiral of platforms**

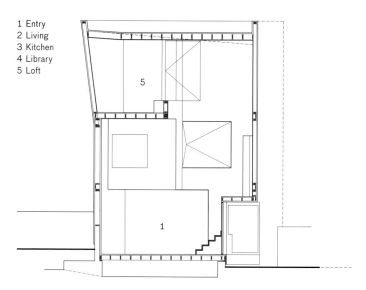

1 Entry
2 Living
3 Kitchen
4 Library
5 Loft

South section

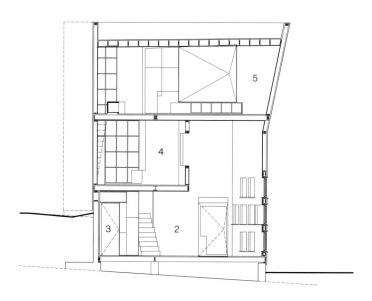

above
**Hinged walls open
all rooms**

opposite
**Vertical library along
stairway**

following spread
**View from Lake
Champlain**

West section ⌐   ⌐ 8'

Turbulence House

Adjacent to adobe courtyard houses
built by the artist Richard Tuttle and the
poet Mei Mei Berssenbrugge, this
small construction is sited atop a windy
desert mesa. The artist's friend Kiki Smith
calls it a "brooch pinned to the mesa."
Its form, imagined like the tip of an iceberg
indicating a much larger form below,
allows turbulent wind to blow through
the center.

    The house was produced in thirty-
two prefabricated parts for two locations
simultaneously—one for the artist couple
in Abiquiu, New Mexico, and one for
an Italian entrepreneur who owns a
sculpture park in Italy.* The interior of
the Abiquiu house is finished according
to local needs and specificities. The
second Turbulence House, made for an
exhibition in Vicenza, Italy, was constructed temporarily inside the Basilica
Palladiana and then moved permanently
to a private sculpture park in Schio,
Italy. The majority of the construction
documents were generated electronically
through three-dimensional computer-
aided-design software. The combination
of prefabricated structures, skin, and local
interior finishes yields a hybrid technique
with connections to the specific sites.

*This was our second prefabricated house design,
the first, was the Z house for Millbrook NY, 1992.

right
Concept watercolor

opposite
**View at mesa entrance
road**

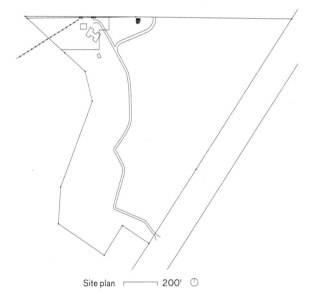

Site plan   200' ⊙

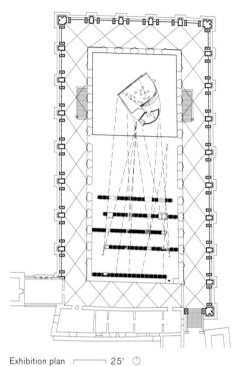

Exhibition plan |————| 25' ⏱

top, right
Construction with prefabricated panels

bottom, right
Moving the Turbulence House into the Basilica Palladiana

opposite, top
Model with roof sloped for optimum solar panel angle

opposite, bottom
Thirty-two prefabricated panels merge structure and skin (by Zahner metals, Kansas City)

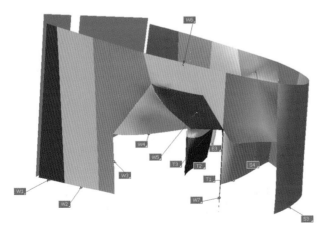

right
Stairway to writing loft and bedroom

opposite
View to east horizon (furniture by Richard Tuttle)

1 Sleeping loft and bath
2 Open to below
3 Study
4 Kitchen
5 Dining
6 Living
7 Storage

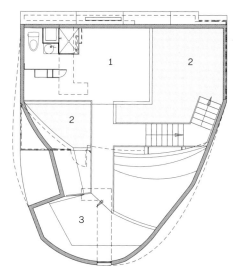

Second-floor plan

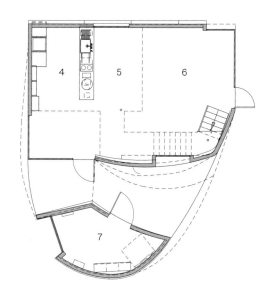

above and opposite
**Kitchen prefabricated
in Austin, Texas**

First-floor plan ⌐―――――┐ 5' ⏱

right
**Kitchen, stairway,
shower**

Turbulence House

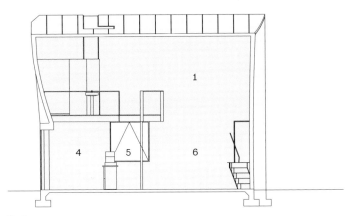

Section

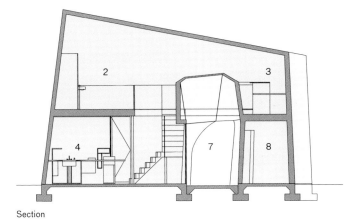

Section

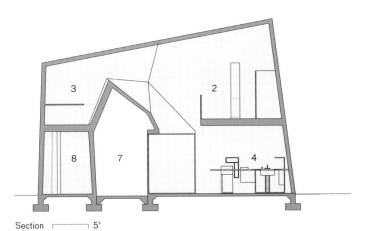

Section ⌐———┐ 5'

1 Sleeping loft beyond
2 Sleeping loft
3 Study
4 Kitchen
5 Dining
6 Living
7 Open breezeway
8 Storage

right
Writing loft, hand plaster work and round edges by local New Mexico craftsmen.

opposite
The desert mesa

right
Turbulence wind portal

opposite
Werner Heisenberg on his deathbed asked God, "Why relativity? And why turbulence?" God, Heisenberg guessed, would only be able to answer the first question.

Tower of Silence

Sited next to three 150-foot-tall Douglas fir trees, which form a vertical, cathedral-like void, this wood-frame studio for painting and writing is sheathed in local natural cedar boards. The 16-square-foot plan is stacked in two rooms of 256 square feet each. The cantilevered porch faces east with Puget Sound, Blake Island, and Seattle in the distance.

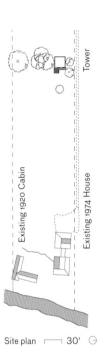

Site plan ⌐ 30'

right
Sketch

opposite
Corner opens to 150-foot-tall Douglas fir trees

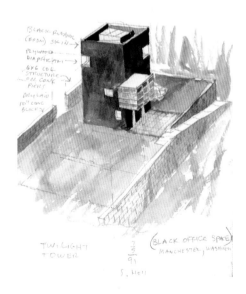

right
**Douglas firs beyond
cedar tower with
a redwood tree at
north facade**

opposite, left
Porch

opposite, right
Staircase

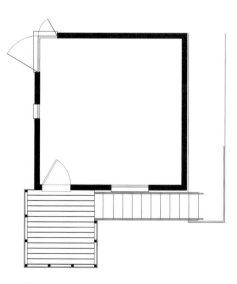

First-floor plan ⌐————⌐ 5' ⊖

above
Built by one carpenter
in 1996 for a total cost
of $17,000

opposite
A geometry of two
stacked cubes; all
wooden construction

Round Lake Hut

Creative and imaginative work begins
in the solitude of the connection of the
mind/eye/hand. This solitary room
with a table and a chair is a functional
drawing studio.

   The wood-framed, 80-square-foot
space, sits on four legs at the edge
of Round Lake. The north and south
elevations are glass in cedar frames.
The sides are black tar paper with
wooden battens. There is a one-by-four-
foot window at the floor facing east
toward the sunrise. There is no plumbing,
no electricity, and no insulation.

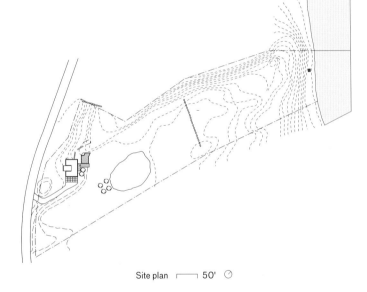

Site plan ⌐──⌐ 50' ⊘

right
**Round Lake, a 10,000-
year-old spring-fed
body of water, is the
focus of the hut.**

opposite
South view

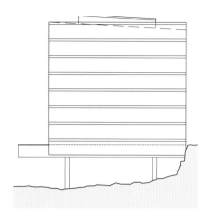

Section

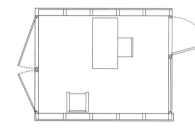

Plan ⌐————————5' ⊙

right
Interior view

opposite
**East-facing window at
level of pine board floor**

Deceleration: A Collapse of Plastic Space

by Michael Bell

The essay "Out of Time and Into Space" by John Hejduk was first published in the journal *Cable* in 1969.[1] It was reprinted and surely more widely read in the context of Hejduk's own compendium of architecture, poems, writing, and interviews—*Mask of Medusa*—published in 1985.[2] Like most of Hejduk's writing, it was partly influenced by an unfolding of space(s)—either architectural or literary. In some sense Hejduk's entire career was played out in this way—the thesis of one Hejduk project was made possible only by the realization of space in the project that preceded it. Conditions were set that once understood could be made newly malleable or more poignantly difficult, tenuous, and at times ineffable. The essay "Out of Time and Into Space" did stand on its own as a ground-breaking interpretation of the work of its subject—Le Corbusier and his Carpenter Center at Harvard University— but the essay never assumed a status equal to Robert Slutzky or Colin Rowe's writing on Le Corbusier even though it observed and delivered as profound a reading of space, and in particular Cubist space in architecture. The essay did, however, serve as a key to understanding Hejduk's work by way of Le Corbusier; it signaled a break in understanding what potentials might be possible if you entered Hejduk's work through a re-reading of Le Corbusier or vice-versa. The same trajectory today leads from Hejduk's work into that of Steven Holl. While the connections Hejduk made to Le Corbusier apply directly to Holl as well, it is perhaps as important to examine how

Hedjuk fabricated his connections to Le Corbusier through writing and to explore the similarity in how Holl also builds his work in and through writing even as he prolifically builds in the literal sense of practice.

It is possible to ask if Hejduk would have pursued an analysis of Le Corbusier's work to the depths that he did if it had not unlocked some aspects of his own architectural production, and similar questions apply to the references provided by Steven Holl in this book. Holl's references to material, site, color, and ultimately to duration, time, and space (in architecture). In the context of this book of houses designed by Holl, it is not a surprise to refer to Hejduk as a foundational figure—a component of Holl's work—and indeed the aspects of work on volume, mass, and space that have always driven Holl's work make him somewhat singular in the degree to which he, like Hejduk, does still cultivate and recast themes that were central in the work of Le Corbusier. Yet well into an era when new means of fabricating architecture that were not available to Le Corbusier—a range of dynamic media systems, semiotic and linguistic controls now half a century past the Carpenter Center, modes of space based in the organizations of attention, rather than the use of literal volume or mass— all of these modes of space in some sense have superceded architecture's deep history of work on mass and volume. Yet Holl, like Hejduk before him, to a surprising degree does still base his work in concepts that can be directly linked back to Le Corbusier; Hejduk's essay on Le Corbusier, however, did add a powerful shift in what might have evolved from the Carpenter Center's achievements, and it seems to have almost not registered on the map of our collective architectural itinerary even as it deeply affected the work of Hejduk and arguably Holl. Both architects have in some ways not fully claimed the breakthroughs they have made—masking them in language that allows concepts to be lodged but not fully understood.

Hejduk's analysis of the Carpenter Center began with what one could see as expected readings of the Carpenter Center as a Cubist work of architecture. Its volumes, spaces, and centrifugal mass—and in particular the temporal organization of the entry procession (its promenade) stands as the passage of time that suggests a somewhat clear evolution of Cubism in architecture. Similar paradigms had proliferated in architectures related to Cubism and Le Corbusier's own production, of course, and Hejduk had crafted architectural exercises designed around Cubist painting in the core studios at Cooper Union; indeed a famous photograph of Hejduk the professor showed him holding a book of Juan Gris's work. Holl's work to date has also been consistently staged in Cubist techniques: see the imploding facets of the Turbulence House, the in-folding surfaces of the Implosion Villa, or the un-framed reflected images in the projected glass of the Little Tesseract House. Holl adds to each of

these circumstances a palpable sense of acceleration and deceleration— these forms are products of motion and gradients of speed and change. For the twenty years prior to the Carpenter Center's emergence, Cubist concepts of simultaneity, implied and literal diagonal tensions, and conflations of central and peripheral generative energies— the core material of Cubist spatial techniques—had been explored widely in architecture and also explicated by Rowe and Slutzky in the context of their *Perspecta* essays on transparency.

The techniques were and are well known, and this has perhaps short circuited or hindered a closer reading of Hejduk's essay and his findings, but more so what invention is still to be found in the connections to and departures from Cubism? Did Hejduk writing about Le Corbusier seem too familiar in 1969 and again in 1985? In this regard you could misread Hejduk as a Cubist architect who was directly relying on Le Corbusier's Cubism. Holl, too, can be easily misread in terms he supplies to the reader; is Holl a phenomenological architect relying on a combination of typology as memory device, and point/line/plane as the means of extending volume and mass— to extend perception as form of parallax? The messages of both architects are far more complex than the antecedent references foster—Hejduk attempted to unfold a reading of the Carpenter Center as a corollary to his own intentions. It was not an illustration of technique or a spatial/historical foundation, but instead a

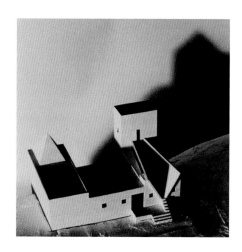

polemic; one which was presented as a form of spatial crisis that seemed to be unheeded despite the obvious reverence paid to Hejduk. Holl and Hejduk intersect sometime around the date of 1985 in the literal context of New York City: "Out of Time and Into Space" is a juncture that when republished in *Mask of Medusa* coincides with the first prominent work by Steven Holl—the Metz House and other small works including the Pool House are completed and presented in relation to theories of typology as they are simultaneously presented as works of spatial abstraction (hence Cubism, El Lisitzky's, etc.) based in planar and linear reading of space. Hejduk's essay on the Carpenter Center similarly masks the potential of what he read in Le Corbusier's work. To understand this, look closely at Hejduk's writing and in particular its suggestion about a limit, or a threshold, to the boundaries of what constituted the accepted plastic qualities of Cubism— and of Cubist space. This is where Holl and Hejduk meet conceptually— the year 1985 and the Manhattan location are the ephemeral locations. Their work does not share formal similarity— or appearances—but in 1985 the spatial attributes, or more accurately the attributes of what can be called a Post-Cubist space—a space that pushed Cubism to unseen limits (rather than simply ceasing to operate within Cubist techniques). It is in some ways a post-plastic space—one based on limits surpassed—and it links these two

architects. The linking occurs by way of the house's program—and by way of space understood in the context of a home.

"Out of Time and Into Space" concludes with the incantation of a potential new space that could be said to emerge as a form of after-effect of Cubism pushed beyond its limits: it is a form of space that Hejduk did not attempt to name but he clearly expressed its possible presence. It was a space that was derived not from allowing Le Corbusier's innovations to stand, but instead by suggesting that they might be toppled or better yet plastically exceeded. Hejduk felt that Le Corbusier had pushed the Cubism he employed at Carpenter Center to its plastic limits; he suggested more than stated that it was possible for a new form of architectural space to emerge at the outer limits of the Carpenter Center's cohesion as a plastic composition. In short the tensions and compression of space in the building's spatial logic had been pushed beyond recoverable limits. In this context is it possible that much of what John Hejduk achieved, and similarly much of what Holl has achieved, is somewhat masked by suggestions that these are architects who continued work begun within the canon of modern space. That they began within the modern movement is clear; so too are the reflections of Cubism as more direct sources—but Hejduk's little-read and thus republished passages provide a key to the depth of his goals and link Hejduk and Holl in a commonly stated, but I think often misunderstood, relationship. "The tension and compression, the push-pull may have therapeutic value to the docile," wrote Hejduk about the Carpenter Center, but "the question remains, at what point do the harmonic fluctuations crack causing dissolution and failure of the spatial organism."[3] Hejduk's text was testing the limits of the composition's Cubist coherence—his analysis described Le Corbusier's spatial enterprise as on the brink of dissolution, and with it the dissolution of a wider and more catastrophic disintegration of the generative plasticity of building spaces. It seems possible, even probable enough that such a comparison requires almost no follow up—Holl's spaces are "soulful," as are Hejduk's. But the comparison is more accurate than people might realize, and it is in this breaking of plastic boundaries that it is more potent and most profitable. Here they are related as architects, but their work is profoundly different in application and evolution. Both have based their most innovative work on exploring a form of space that did not so much alter the course of cubism or replace its techniques; instead they have pushed it to some unresolvable limits and built a new architecture and space in the aftermath—they have occupied a form of space and used it as the source to build new concepts.

It is of course possible to view the work of Steven Holl independently— as separate from his writing and his influences and colleagues—no one has built such a deeply independent collection of houses in half a century. Yet Holl works in ways that are similar to Hejduk, and the comparison brings certain key themes to light. Holl, like Hejduk, has continually provided his reader with a listing of his influences; self-provided directions offered in a shorthand poetic writing style, they usually are based as part semiotic, yet equal, incantations of physics and the material. Holl's writing is part description of building process and materials, part description of program and use— often based in themes of everyday life and use, they also are poignantly existential and as such it is houses that have been some of his most successful works. Holl firmly ties words and concepts to material and to space—ultimately to perception and to a user who has often been understood as a kind of latter-day humanist subject—someone who is held comfortably in the directness of lived experience. Holl, like Hejduk, seems to strive to create a literary equivalent to the actual experience of his built works—here material and space are not only described but become palpable and take on attributes of weight and mass more than sign or signal. In this volume Holl's text is titled "Black Swan Theory"—his writing refers to a wide range of themes and more complex attributes of space that his phrases strive to condense; the ambitions of his architecture when printed in books are carried in part by photographs, in part by words—always both.

In "Black Swan Theory" see his terms such as "Porous Light," "Chromatic Duration," "Site: Maximum Compression."

These titles are highly specific and indeed are presented in the book as literal experiments and didactic exercises— yet ultimately if their poetic role as spatial concepts is to be imagined as much as actually lived as built works, that forces the reader to become the author of the qualities of space that Holl only instigates. They beg to be realized in physical space, and they are in his houses—but what, for example, is "porous light?" Is it light with holes in it? Can light have a hole in it? Holl, in some way it seems, would prefer we understand the phenomena more than actually witness it in his houses—he has frequently stated he likes ideas more than buildings. In "Black Swan Theory" Holl offers a means to play out the experiment in Porous Light separate from his houses. He writes: "To see this phenomenon, simply hold a perforated plane immediately in front of a piece of blank paper then move it farther away gradually." The experiment yields a gradually softening shadow edge—it is space, not so much light, that has holes in it—light forms a hole in the spaces. Yet if the space itself is light as we slowly realize it is, and it is light forming the holes then indeed this is porous light or light with holes in it. The improbable but ultimately powerful phrase leads to comprehension—slowly. Holl's space seems non-plastic—unframed, and in Hejduk's words, dissolute—positive and negative volumes are here relieved of their compositional dialectics and historical authority—space now has holes in it, light is penetrating light, and the edges

of the expected holes or figure/ground (the shadows) are not distinct or at all persistent but instead varied and gradient. What aspect of modern dialectics remains here? Some formal figures to be sure, but the spaces are still new today and as unexplored as they were when Holl first began to make his breakthrough works.

John Hejduk also offered carefully titled spatial themes when his work was formally presented and published. Hejduk's writing and his spatial references and phrases, like Holl's, are deeply influential in their own right; that is, they portend qualities of space even without providing literal examples. In Hejduk's writing there are terms that seem to have strong parallels to those of Holl. References to color by Hejduk suggest a "'density' of pigmentation"; references to space offer an image of "harmonic fluctuations" and "dissolution." Hejduk wrote numerous times of turning space "inside out." Hejduk's spatial ambitions, perhaps more than his actual architectural works, provide insight into Holl's architectural goals—more so than any other architect. These are works that are derived from an exploration of mass and material after it is unframed—after a spatial operation has opened space as it re-densifies matter. In the houses published here Holl gives space physical properties, and like Hejduk it is a concept of thought made physical that often is asked to produce architectural space. In "Black Swan Theory" Holl writes that "maximum compression of architectural thought might yield domestic simplicity." A house can be the "spatial representation of an idea" writes Holl—his work is intended to be understood as it is occupied.

Though Holl refers to a house as "vessel," he sees the vessel as a container within which phenomena yield challenges to the very stability of the enclosed space. Passages of time leave only the "existential objects of life." Holl has written continually about the need to anchor architecture to site, yet he has continually unfolded the spaces he creates and he has remained existential about the project of producing an interior—of making a house. Holl's vessels themselves remain (they must as architecture) but it is the duration of that life that is the work's reality; the persistence of material itself under transformation is a clue to this ultimate goal. His Turbulence House is perhaps the most potent example of this to date—the "domestic simplicity" that remains as the facades fold inward in all directions, sculpting an exterior torus space that passes through the building, is adjacent to the massive energy witnessed in the building facade and mass. More so these facades exhibit a tendency to both fold inward and remain flat—this is not the ruled surfaces and the smooth transitions of prefabrication or manufactured surfaces often discussed today. Instead this building only reluctantly produces interior volumes by way of curvatures that seem to prefer flatness; the curves no doubt do produce a full-bodied plastic form but they do so from a series of striated and ribbed surfaces that recall a lineage of flattened and simultaneously curved

spaces; they recall Cézanne to Braque, dealing with problems of depth and flatness, but also produce an interior for living, a space that is within, or perhaps more accurately, beside the tensioned work of the facades.

Holl has frequently invoked a sense of place and site in his work—and he has always posited works with the eye, and the body of a witness; a slowed presence whose experience dilates space, and is dilated by space—an opening is made in an otherwise tight and continuous envelope of space. But Holl has also continually pushed space to its elastic limits—planar spaces that never provide depth leave the body unescorted (see the Planar House and indeed much of his work with planar space); volumes are stacked to imply weight but are hollowed out from within to suspend mass but imply collapse of the volumes that their emptiness encloses. Rooms are flooded (see the Stretto House) to reveal their prior emptiness or our inability to occupy them; bodies are carefully positioned, but the full occupation of space requires constant movement—or an intuition based in duration.

Holl's references to history are less overt, and far fewer than Hejduk's. They seem less exacting in terms of specificity to the architect, and his book is less of a compendium than Hejduk's. He is also less willing to operate exactly from an architecturally historical vantage; instead, I would argue he has resorted to a poetic but intuitively potent form of physics to express his concepts of space.

Yet of architects working today it seems that Holl, like Hejduk, would welcome the stories of Le Corbusier or Mies van der Rohe to the debate about his work, and his work persists in operating at its most experimental at the edge of evolutions that begin still in modern space.

Holl leaves clues about his intentions in various ways, though; texts that often reveal a connection to astronomy and physics also speak as much to the everyday. Weight persists in his work as a knowable presence, but it is often pushed to find its bearing against an unknown plateau—he invokes the framed knowledge of material as well as spatial limits—Holl deconstructs as well as constructs the verifiability of material. Light folds into itself as often it is revealed against a solid or fixed form in Holl's work—weight that has been alleviated is first shown and then removed—these attributes are revealed via the slow occupation of use. As he notes this is uniquely possible in a house and perhaps not so in a public building. Like Hejduk this is an architecture based in perception—but it is based in perception at its limits—perception that must exceed the location of the body and enter the wider space that has no limits.

Hejduk's text was in some ways an unmet challenge—it was the "docile" that he suggested might find "therapeutic" comfort in the reciprocity of push and pull—in the joining of plastic space; but it was those willing to press the dialectic to extremes and past that he invoked but did not quite describe. What were the uses of this space? My own relation to Steven Holl's and to John Hejduk's work is based in this pushing past plastic limits; here spaces can be turned inside out, bodies as the visible denominator of a presumed latter-day humanism (at least in Holl's case) are indeed vividly present here. But if they are not in crisis, they are in some troubled yet ecstatic place: Holl writes that the "internal core of a room is a reverie" in this book. He is suggesting that at the core of a room's emptiness is a space derived not from the bounding closure of its walls but from its deep but absent source of palpable energy. Holl's Pool House and the Planar House are examples that unfold an idea across twenty years—planes that relieve space as much as momentarily join it. These are spaces generated as frames are withdrawn, as space is imploding. The Hejduk analysis of the Carpenter Center was written at least ten years before Holl's work emerged in the press— and Holl's early work was formally based in rural and urban typologies (not the Corbusian syntax of the New York Five)— but Holl and Hejduk share the closest consistency in how space is conceived in a post-Corbusian era. If work by Charles Gwathmey and Peter Eisenman or Michael Graves shared the syntax and even the semiotic tautology that Manfredo Tafuri enunciated in "the Five" it was actually Holl who more closely shared a concept of space and indeed moved a concept of space past the historical antecedents of Cubism's alluvial and viscous presence.[4] These adjectives refer to the writing of Robert Slutzky; but here they stand in as a

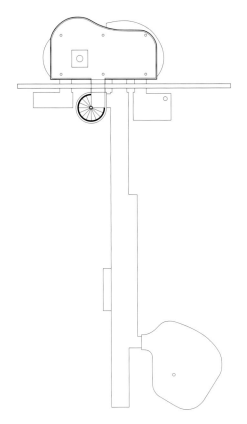

less complex reference to space that is as Hejduk stated "harmonic" and witnessed as fluctuations in a continuous field. Holl's work, I would argue, has actually often done the opposite; it has drained space of its palpable viscosity and instead revealed in space moments of uneasy turbulence— topological turns to space that trouble comprehension based on easily identified frames or clear material physics. In an era where architecture is more frequently understood as an attribute of larger and more mobile and virtual forms of power (i.e., economics) to involve architectural space (as volume and mass) in these a-plastic moments is difficult, perception is to reassert architecture's ability to speak even against the most troubled circumstances of its own weakness.

My understanding of Hejduk and Holl's work was situated at the conflation of their writing but also against the backdrop of Hejduk's Diamond and Wall houses. *Mask of Medusa* was published as Steven Holl's Pool House (actually a form of wall house according to Holl) and the generational aspect of their relationship was diminished. Hejduk's work after the Carpenter Center essay was now fully a decided form of post-Cubist composition. It was still work that took the form of a still life, but it now stood in front of the picture plane and the work found its plastic resonance without the easy sourcing of a bounding frame. In the case of Holl and of Hejduk you found yourself continually looking at the periphery of their drawings—at the surreal aspects of the drawn trees, the furniture and everyday

things shown in the spaces, and ultimately at the literal or imagined extended landscape of internal and external space. Here Holl invokes and relies on the immediate to create the extended. Holl quoted Emerson early in his career to give context to his goals: "the eye never tires so long as it can see the horizon."[5] He consistently reaffirms the interiority of each work, showing us a city of atomized lives, interiors, and private stillness— yet he also places the comprehension of space into a wider expanded landscape. Holl's horizons are topological even as his buildings are often typological. Just as likely to derive expansion by way of compression, they are also as likely to open vistas by closing down vision and instead creating material depth. These are forms of architectural space that are at their core forms of spatial comprehension. You do of course occupy the space of a Holl building, but it is the means by which these spaces, like Hejduk's, portend extending horizons that gives them deep value. These works provide vision that returns to a late modern subject a quotient of weight and time that verifies their presence, and also undermines the power of commodity procedures as the predominant organizer of contemporary space. Hejduk and Holl do recoil from the "therapeutic"—they do leave the subject very much on his own and seeking a new set of social relations, communications born of the new conditions.

Certainly a sense of melancholy is in this work, but ultimately I think it is a sense of weighted and corporeal subjectivity that is implied and realized here—it is, as Holl writes, a form of reverie. It is the precision of Holl's formal work and his tectonics that give these spaces their amazing palpability—but, like Hejduk, it is Holl's teaching, his writing, and the degree to which his architecture is the source of his insights that is most of value. This is perhaps what invites the comparison between Holl and Hejduk but ultimately between Holl and Le Corbusier as the ambition of the work is based in the degree to which space and perception are capable of carrying tremendous ambitions for social life. It is the concept of space that precedes all work—written or architectural. It is the effect of space and the means by which it is ultimately perceived if not born of a perceiving subject. In the end this means that architecture instigates changes in perception, but that perception then changes the intuited limits of space— we exit the expected boundaries of time— and enter space.

It is both harrowing and thrilling, but it is ultimately the only possibility after the limits of the harmonic fluctuation have been passed—we are no longer able to be docile. The normal attributes of a still life are here infused with properties of acceleration and deceleration as limits are approached. Hesitancy sustains a pause for fear of elastic limits passed, and finally boundaries are irrecoverably crossed. A center is voided; a new terrain opens at the former outer edge of space and, as Holl has so often written, a place is revealed.

1. John Hejduk, "Out of Time and Into Space," *Cable* (1969).

2. John Hejduk, *Mask of Medusa: Works 1947–1983* (New York: Rizzoli Press, 1985).

3. Ibid.

4. Manfredo Tafuri, "European Graffiti: Five × Five = Twenty-Five," *Oppositions* 5 (Summer 1976): 41.

5. Ralph Waldo Emerson, "Nature," in *Essays* (New York: Westvaco, 1978).

opposite
Golden section detail

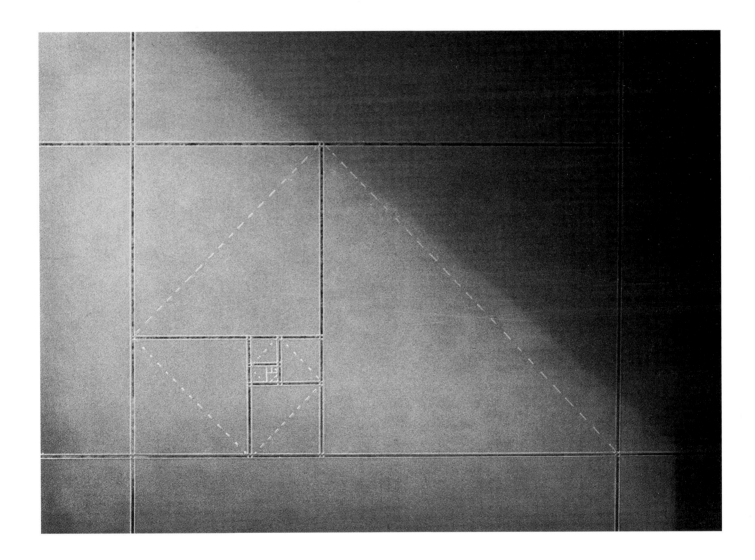

Project Credits

The Swiss Residence
2001–2006

location
Washington, D.C., USA
program
residence including living spaces
for ambassador, staff quarters, and
representational spaces
client
Swiss Federal Office for Buildings
and Logistics [BBL]
design architects
Steven Holl (SHA) and Justin Ruessli
(Ruessli Architekten AG)
associates in charge
Stephen O'Dell, Tim Bade (SHA)
project architects
Olaf Schmidt (SHA) and Mimi Kueh (RA)
project team
Arnault Biou, Peter Englaender,
Annette Goderbauer, Li Hu, Irene Vogt
(SHA), and Andreas Gervasi,
Phillip Röösli, Rafael Schnyder,
Urs Zuercher (RA)
structural engineers
A. F. Steffen Engineers, Robert
Silman Associates, P.C.
mechanical engineers
B+B Energietechnik AG, B2E
Consulting Engineers
interior designer
ZedNetwork Hannes Wettstein
landscape architect
Robert Gissinger

Stretto House
1989–1991

location
Dallas, Texas, USA
program
private residence
client
withheld
design architect
Steven Holl
project architect
Adam Yarinsky
project team
Peter Lynch, Bryan Bell, Mathew Karlen,
William Wilson, Stephen Cassell,
Kent Hikida, Florian Schmidt,
Thomas Jenkinson, Lucinda Knox
local architect
Max Levy, Dallas
structural consultant
Datum Engineering
mechanical consultant
Interfield Engineering
contractor
Thomas S. Byrne Construction
landscape consultant
Kings Creek Landscaping

Writing With Light House
2001–2004

location
Long Island, New York, USA
program
private residence
client
withheld
design architect
Steven Holl
project architect
Annette Goderbauer
project team
Martin Cox, Irene Vogt, Christian
Wassmann
structural engineers
Silman Associates, P.C.
general contractors
Koral Bros. Inc.

Oceanic Retreat
2001

location
Kauai'i, Hawaii, USA
program
private residence
client
withheld
design architect
Steven Holl
project architect
Martin Cox
project team
Arnault Biou, Jason Frantzen,
Steve O'Dell, Olaf Schmidt
local architect
Peter Vincent & Associates
engineers
Guy Nordenson and Associates
contractors
Krekow-Jennings Inc.
(Steve Farrell, PM)

Porosity House
2005–

location
Southampton, New York, USA
program
weekend house
client
withheld
design architect
Steven Holl
project architect
Rodolfo Dias
project team
Cosimo Caggiula, Ernest Ng

Sun Slice House
2005–

location
Lake Garda, Italy
program
private residence
client
withheld
design architect
Steven Holl
project architect
Alessandro Orsini
project team
Francesco Bartolozzi

Y House
1997–1999

location
Catskills, New York, USA
program
weekend retreat
design architect
Steven Holl
project architect
Erik Langdalen
project team
Annette Goderbauer, Yoh Hanaoka,
Brad Kelley, Justin Korhammer,
Jennifer Lee, Chris McVoy
local architect
Peter Liaunig
structural engineers
Robert Silman Associates, P.C.
lighting consultants
L'Observatoire International
contractor
Dick Dougherty
furniture
Face Design

Planar House
2002–2005

location
Arizona, USA
program
private residence
client
withheld
design architect
Steven Holl
project architect
Martin Cox (Tim Bade, Schematic Design)
project team
Robert Edmonds, Annette Goderbauer,
Hideki Hirahara, Clark Manning
general contractors
The Construction Zone
structural engineers
Rudow & Berry
mechanical engineer
Roy Otterbein
civil engineers
Fleet Fisher
electrical engineers
Associated Engineering
landscape architect
Steve Martino & Associates

House at Martha's Vineyard
1984–1988

location
Martha's Vineyard, Massachusetts, USA
program
private residence
design architect
Steven Holl
project architect
Peter Lynch
project team
Stephen Cassell, Ralph Nelson,
Peter Shinoda
structural engineer
Robert Lawson
contractor
Doyle Construction
custom steel/brass work
Alvin Cooke Metal Works

Implosion Villa
1992

location
The Hague, The Netherlands
program
private residence
design architect
Steven Holl
project team
Janet Cross, Mario Gooden,
Terry Surjan, Tomoaki Tanaka

Little Tesseract
2001

location
Rhinebeck, New York, USA
program
solarstack prototype
design architects
Steven Holl, Solange Fabião
project architect
Chris Otterbine, Laura Sansone
project team
Makram El-Kadi, Anderson Lee,
Christian Wassmann, Urs Vogt
fabricator
The Orchard Group

Nail Collector's House
2001–2004

location
Essex, New York, USA
program
private residence
client
G. Alan Wardle
design architect
Steven Holl
project architect
Stephen O'Dell
structural engineers
Silman Associates, PC.
fabricator
Mitch Rabinew

Turbulence House
2001–2004

location
New Mexico, USA
program
guest house
client
R. Tuttle and M. Berssenbrugge
design architect
Steven Holl
project architects
Anderson Lee, Richard Tobias
project team
Arnault Biou, Matt Johnson
local architect
Kramer E. Woodard Architects
structural engineers
Delapp Engineering
metal panel fabricators
A. Zahner Company

Tower of Silence
1992

location
Manchester, Washington, USA
program
architectural retreat
design architect
Steven Holl
project team
Janet Cross, Todd Fouser
fabricator
Ray Lorio

Round Lake Hut
2001

location
Rhinebeck, New York, USA
program
watercolor retreat
design architect
Steven Holl
fabricator
The Orchard Group

Bibliography of Published Writings and Monographs

Holl, Steven. *Hybrid Instrument*. Iowa City: The University of Iowa School of Art and Art History, 2006.

———. *Luminosity/Porosity*. Tokyo, Japan: Noto Shappan, 2006.

———. "Alvar Aalto: Villa Mairea, Noormarkku / Porosity to Fusion." In *Entrez Lentement*, edited by Lorenzo Gaetani, 186–207. Milan: Lotus Eventi, 2005.

———. *Steven Holl*. Edited by Ji-seong Jeong. *Contemporary Architecture* 62. Korea: CA Press, 2005.

———. *Experiments in Porosity*. Edited by Brian Carter and Annette W. LeCuyer. Buffalo: University at Buffalo, School of Architecture and Planning, 2005.

———. *Simmons Hall*. Edited by Todd Gannon. Source Books in Architecture, vol. 5. New York: Princeton Architectural Press, 2004.

———. *Steven Holl: Competitions*. Edited by Yoshio Futugawa. *GA Document* 82. Japan: A.D.A. Edita Tokyo, 2004.

———. *Steven Holl*. Edited by Francesco Garofolo. New York: Universe-Rizzoli, 2003.

———. *Steven Holl 1986–2003*. Edited by Fernando Marquez Cecilia and Richard Levene. Madrid: El Croquis Editorial, 2003.

———. *Steven Holl Architect*. Milan: Electa Architecture, 2002.

———. *Idea and Phenomena*. Edited by Architekturzentrum Wien. Baden: Lars Müller Publishers, 2002.

———. *Written in Water*. Baden: Lars Müller Publishers, 2002.

———. *Steven Holl 1998–2002: thought, matter and experience* [*El Croquis* 108]. Madrid: El Croquis Editorial, 2001.

———. "Density in the Landscape." In *City Fragments: Seven Strategies for Making an Urban Fragment in the Hudson Valley*. Columbia Books of Architecture. New York: Columbia University Press, 2001.

———. *Parallax*. New York: Princeton Architectural Press, 2000.

———. *The Chapel of St. Ignatius*. New York: Princeton Architectural Press, 1999.

———. *Steven Holl 1996–1999*. Edited by Fernando Marquez Cecilia and Richard Levene [*El Croquis* 93]. Madrid: El Croquis Editorial, 1999.

———. "Intertwining With the City: Museum of Contemporary Art in Helsinki." *Harvard Architectural Review* 10 (1998).

———. *Kiasma*. Helsinki: The Finnish Building Center, 1998.

———. *Exactness of Doubt*. Pamphlet Architecture, vols. 1–10. New York: Princeton Architectural Press, 1998.

———. "Twofold Meaning." *Kenchiku Bunka* 52, Aug. 1997.

———. *Intertwining: Selected Projects 1989–1995*. New York: Princeton Architectural Press, 1996.

———. *Steven Holl 1986–1996*. Edited by Fernando Marquez Cecilia and Richard Levine [*El Croquis* 78]. Madrid: El Croquis Editorial, 1996.

———. *Stretto House: Steven Holl Architects*. New York: Monacelli Press, 1996.

———. *Steven Holl*. Interview with Yushio Futagawa. Edited by Yukio Futagawa. *GA Document Extra*. Japan: A.D.A. Edita Tokyo, 1996.

———. "Pre-Theoretical Ground." In *D: Columbia Documents of Architecture and Theory* 4, edited by Bernard Tschumi, 27–59. New York: Columbia University Graduate School of Architecture, Planning and Preservation, 1995.

———. "Questions of Perception." *A & U Tokyo* 2.94 (Apr. 1994): 25–28. (New edition 2006 William Stout Architectural Books)

———. "Intertwining / Verweben." In *Color of an Architect*, 12–57. Hamburg: Galerie Fur Architektur, 1994. (exhibition catalog)

——. *Steven Holl*. Zurich: Artemis Zurich and Bordeaux: arc en reve centre d'architecture, 1993. (exhibition catalog)

——. *Edge of a City*. Pamphlet Architecture, vol. 13. New York: Princeton Architectural Press, 1991.

——. *Anchoring: Selected Projects 1975–1988*. New York: Princeton Architectural Press, 1989.

——. "Within the City: Phenomena of Relations." In *Design Quarterly*, vol. 139. Cambridge, Massachusetts: MIT Press, 1988. (exhibition catalog)

——. "Teeter Totter Principles." In *Perspecta* 21. New Haven: Yale University Press, 1984.

——. "Foundations: American House Types." In *Precis* IV, edited by Sheryl Kolasinski and P.A. Morton. New York: Columbia University Press, 1983.

——. *Rural and Urban House Types*. Pamphlet Architecture, vol. 9. New York: William Stout Architectural Books, 1982.

——. *Anatomy of a Skyscraper: Cities, the Forces that Shape Them*. Edited by Liza Taylor. New York: Cooper-Hewitt Museum, 1982.

——. "Conversation with Alberto Sartoris." *Archetype* (Fall 1982).

——. *Bridge of Houses*. Pamphlet Architecture, vol. 7. New York: William Stout Architectural Books, 1981.

——. *The Alphabetical City*. Pamphlet Architecture, vol. 5. New York: Pamphlet Architecture Press, 1980.

——. "USSR in the USA." *Skyline* (May 1979).

——. "The Desert De Retz." Student Quarterly Syracuse. New York: Syracuse School of Architecture, 1978.

——. Rev. of *The Blue Mountain Conference*. *Skyline*, Nov. 1978.

——. *Bridges*. Pamphlet Architecture, vol. 1. New York: Pamphlet Architecture Press, 1977.

Acknowledgments

Architecture is the most fragile of
arts: These works depended on great
collaboration of all the energetic
and creative people listed with each
of the projects of this book: from clients,
and consultants to the architects in
our office.

Special thanks to: Solange Fabião,
and Michael Bell, Molly Blieden,
Priscilla Fraser, Hollyamber Kennedy,
David van der Leer, Kevin C. Lippert,
Ruth W. Lo, Adam Michaels, Lauren
Nelson Packard, Yehuda Safran, Brett
Snyder, and Christina Yessios

Image Credits

Published by
Princeton Architectural Press
37 East Seventh Street
New York, New York 10003

For a free catalog of books, call 1.800.722.6657.
Visit our web site at www.papress.com.

Book design by Project Projects

For Princeton Architectural Press
Edited by Lauren Nelson Packard

Special thanks to Nettie Aljian, Dorothy Ball, Nicola
Bednarek, Janet Behning, Becca Casbon, Penny
(Yuen Pik) Chu, Russell Fernandez, Wendy Fuller,
Jan Haux, John King, Nancy Eklund Later, Linda Lee,
Katharine Myers, Scott Tennent, Jennifer Thompson,
Joseph Weston, and Deb Wood of Princeton
Architectural Press —Kevin C. Lippert, publisher

For Steven Holl Architects
Production by David van der Leer, Priscilla Fraser,
and Christina Yessios

Library of Congress Cataloging-in-Publication Data
Holl, Steven.
    House : black swan theory / Steven Holl.—1st ed.
        p. cm.
    Includes bibliographical references.
    ISBN-13: 978-1-56898-587-9 (alk. paper)
    ISBN-10: 1-56898-587-8 (alk. paper)
1. Holl, Steven. 2. Architecture, Domestic—United
States—20th century. 3. Architecture, Domestic—United
States—21st century. I. Title.
    NA737.H56A4 2007
    728'.37092—dc22
                    2006032629